Adaptive Leadership

Navigating Change in Today's Business World

Dr. Ty H. Wenglar, PhD

ISBN: 979-8-89324-446-5

The Lionfish Press

5100 Long Arrow Canyon

Bee Cave, TX 78738

info@wenglargroup.com

Acknowledgments

To my parents, Buck and Lisa Wenglar and Sandi Richards, who planted the seeds of curiosity and love for learning in me. Thank you for teaching me the value of education and for being my constant source of motivation and encouragement.

In the loving memory of my grandmother, Myrtle "Totsie" Wenglar, whose support and belief in my potential were unwavering.

Dedication

To my beloved wife.

Cathy, you have been my rock, enduring the long hours and absences, managing our household, caring for our children with unwavering dedication, and ensuring our home was a place of peace and progress. Your ability to juggle countless responsibilities while being my steadfast supporter is nothing short of miraculous. I am forever grateful for your love, patience, and sacrifice.

Table of Contents

About the Author

Dr. Ty H. Wenglar is an accomplished construction executive and scholar in Organizational Leadership with extensive experience in multi-family development and construction. Renowned for his player-coach leadership style and a proactive, results-oriented mindset, Dr. Wenglar is actively involved in academic and community leadership roles. He has a passion for teaching, mentoring, and conducting research in leadership ethics and practices.

Dr. Wenglar's academic focus lies at the intersection of leadership ethics and organizational effectiveness, focusing on how foundational ethical principles like the Golden Rule influence leadership styles across different cultural and organizational contexts. His doctoral dissertation, "Exploring the Intersection of Ethical and Virtuous Leadership: An Analysis of Correlation and Interchangeability of Measurement Tools," investigates the measurable impact of ethical and virtuous leadership traits on organizational outcomes.

Additionally, Dr. Wenglar's research delves into the application of ethical principles in leadership, seeking to enhance both theoretical and practical understanding of how aligning organizational purposes with ethical leadership can foster environments of compassion and integrity. Through his extensive experience and academic contributions, Dr. Wenglar continues to inspire leaders to embrace ethical practices and create positive, lasting impacts in their organizations and communities.

Note to Readers

Dear Reader,

Thank you for picking up this book on leadership. I want to address something you might notice right away: the book's size. This book is shorter than the industry average, about 25% shorter, in fact. You may wonder why, and I believe the reason is an essential part of what makes these books unique and, more importantly, valuable.

I do not consider myself a writer. I do not write for a living, nor do I aspire to become a full-time author. Instead, I write to share the knowledge and experiences I've accumulated over the last four decades. My journey has taken me from a common laborer to a corporate executive, from a lowly private in the US Army to various roles in between. Along the way, I have earned an undergraduate degree, an MBA, and finally, a PhD in Organizational Leadership. Despite my academic achievements, I have never worked in academia, and I consider this a positive.

Many prestigious leadership scholars, while knowledgeable, often lack real-world experience. They might not fully understand the complexities and challenges that come with leadership in practical, everyday situations. My background is firmly rooted in the realities of the workplace, from the ground floor to the boardroom. This perspective allows me to provide practical advice and strategies that are immediately applicable.

The brevity of my books is intentional. I want to respect your time by getting straight to the point and providing you with actionable insights without the fluff. In the fast-paced world of business, I believe that concise, impactful information is more valuable than long-winded theoretical discussions. These books are designed to be read quickly, absorbed easily, and applied immediately.

Thank you for choosing to spend your valuable time with my work. I hope you find these books to be a useful and practical guide on your own leadership journey.

Sincerely,

Dr. Ty H. Wenglar

Foreward

The essay that served as the genesis of this book.

ACADEMIA Letters

Failure to Adapt

Ty Wenglar, Southeastern University

Citation: Wenglar, T. (2021). Failure to Adapt. *Academia Letters*, Article 3240. https://doi.org/10.20935/AL3240.

An Internet search of "What is the most pressing issue in leadership today?" will yield just over 600 million results. In reading the top 15 to 20 articles and reports, a variety of common themes appear. Issues such as attracting and retaining top talent, a lack of understanding/alignment with the company vision, and managerial effectiveness appear in virtually every article on the subject. When reading and researching such a topic, one must ask, are these actually the problems, or are these the visible symptoms of a deeper underlying issue? By utilizing the three previous example issues in a thorough comparison from asynchronous perspectives, it can be concluded that the answer to this question is absolutely. All of these issues can be distilled down to a single underlying issue: the failure to adapt to an ever-changing business environment and workforce.

The first issue of attracting and retaining top talent is an extremely apropos example. Viewed from an employee's opportunity perspective, as stated by Dana Manciagli (2016), "in- demand professionals have more opportunities today, [and] it's harder to recruit and retain top performers."

From a human resources perspective, as it relates to benefits, compensation, and company culture, an employee's decision to join or leave an organization is rooted in the company's adaptation to changes in the marketplace, which influences said decision (Manciagli, 2016). Rigorous structure is an organization's worst enemy in this case because it limits the company's ability to adapt. It is not employees' current compensation that causes them to begin looking for alternatives. It is how that compensation compares to changes in the market as a whole.

To press on in the face of difficulty, organizations and leaders must have a "North Star" (i.e., a core purpose they strongly believe in that anchors a given organizational initiative and guides their decision-making (Dallas, 2015). This "star" is typically embedded in the company's vision and mission. Sadly, a company's vision is often used as a marketing and public relations tool rather than a guiding principle for management. Just as organizations are constantly evolving, an organization's vision should also be evolving. Organizations, especially large ones, have a natural tendency to follow established patterns of behavior—even in response to dramatic environmental shifts. Stuck in the antiquated modes of thinking and working that brought success in the past, market leaders simply accelerate all their tried-and- true activities. In trying to dig themselves out of a hole, they just deepen it (Sull, 1999). The primary failure here is that the organization does not alter its vision and, therefore, its course based on those dramatic shifts in the business environment. The most powerful visions are end-user-focused and simple for everyone to understand. An unfortunate paradox is that the simpler the vision is, the more complicated it is to implement. Making things easy for your end customers means that leaders have to cross many turfs and break down silo walls within and outside the organization (Dallas, 2015).

Organizational or initiative success is largely rooted in the managerial effectiveness of the leader. To survive and thrive, every organization must know how to navigate change. Sadly, 75% of change initiatives fail, according to a recent study by McKinsey & Co. (Dallas, 2015). Although the actual change is often blamed, this failure is not the result of the change itself but the leader's ability to understand, implement, and adapt to the change. A 2007 survey by the Society for Human Resource Management showed that three of the top four obstacles and challenges during major organizational changes are directly impacted and led by the leadership and managers of the organization (Benedict, 2007). In addition to a leader's impact on managing change, today's business environment is witnessing the beginning of a dramatic shift in the mindset and mentality of leaders. Most people, including many leaders, think of leaders as the people in charge—the decision-makers, the authority. Yet, another approach is to view the leader as performing a service for the group or team—in other words, they act as servant leaders. This is actually an old concept with roots in Confucian philosophy. The modern version of servant leadership was conceptualized by Robert Greenleaf, who worked for almost 40 years at AT&T. Greenleaf argued that to develop a successful, high-functioning team or organization, leaders are obliged to make followers' welfare and well-being priorities and to serve followers by providing for their needs and responding to their concerns (as cited in Riggio, 2018). This philosophy is best communicated in Greenleaf's quote, "The organization exists for the person as much as the person exists for the organization" (as cited in Riggio, 2018). Although Robert Greenleaf's ideas were presented almost 50 years ago, it is the "millennial" mindset and personality of today's young professionals that have highlighted the need to adapt to (or at least have an understanding of) a servant style of leadership.

There are myriad issues and challenges facing today's leaders. Some are extremely specific to a given organization or situation, whereas others affect virtually all organizations. In today's business environment, the vast majority of these issues can be distilled down to a single challenge: the need to adapt to an ever-changing environment. Although the failure to adapt to market shifts manifests itself in a variety of ways, depending on the respective industry and the adaptation that is needed, adaptation remains the single greatest challenge facing today's leaders.

References

Benedict, A. (2007). *2007 change management survey report.* Alexandria, VA: Society for Human Resource Management.

Dallas, H. J. (2015, October 22). Here are 4 ways leaders can deal with change. *Fortune.*

Retrieved from http://fortune.com/2015/10/22/change-leaders-managers/

Manciagli, D. (2016, April 13). 4 biggest challenges facing business leaders today. *Biz Journals.* Retrieved from https://www.bizjournals.com/bizjournals/how-to/growth-strategies/ 2016/04/4-biggest-challenges-facing-business-leaders-today.html

Riggio, R. E. (2018, December 9). What is servant leadership and why does it matter? [web log]. *Psychology Today.* Retrieved from https://www.psychologytoday.com/us/blog/ cutting-edge-leadership/201812/what-is-servant-leadership-and-why-does-it-matter

Sull, D. (1999, July-August). Why good companies go bad. *Harvard Business Review*, 42–55. Retrieved from https://hbr.org/1999/07/why-good-companies-go-bad

CHAPTER 1

The Changing Dynamics of Talent Acquisition

Personal Narrative: The Changing Dynamics of Talent Acquisition

When I started at ABC, they had also just hired a new head of HR at ABC Tech, who quickly realized our traditional recruitment methods were failing. The construction industry was evolving, and we struggled to attract top talent. Our reliance on job ads and waiting for applications wasn't working.

A turning point came during a meeting with all of the division heads and executive team, who stressed the urgency of revamping our strategy. We decided to leverage social media and actively engage potential candidates on platforms like LinkedIn and GitHub. Attending industry events and tech meetups also became crucial. Networking and showcasing our company's culture in person allowed us to connect with passive candidates.

We also improved our employer brand by sharing engaging content about our innovative projects and inclusive culture. Implementing an employee referral program expanded our reach and brought in candidates who fit well culturally.

However, an initial mistake was underestimating the time and effort required for this proactive approach. We stretched our team thin and nearly missed critical hiring deadlines. It was a hard lesson in the need for adequate resources and planning.

Ultimately, this new strategy paid off, attracting high-quality candidates and speeding up our hiring process. The experience taught me the importance of adaptability and thorough preparation in talent acquisition.

Introduction

The landscape of talent acquisition is evolving at an unprecedented pace. In today's business environment, companies face significant challenges in attracting and retaining top talent. This chapter delves into the modern workforce trends, analyzing how organizations can adapt to these changes to remain competitive. By examining case studies of successful and unsuccessful talent acquisition strategies, we aim to provide practical insights for leaders navigating this dynamic landscape.

Modern Workforce Trends

The modern workforce is characterized by shifting expectations and values. Today's employees prioritize factors such as work-life balance, meaningful work, and opportunities for professional growth over traditional incentives like salary and job security (Manciagli, 2016). This shift has been particularly pronounced among younger generations, such as Millennials and Generation Z, who seek more than just a paycheck from their employers.

One significant trend is the increasing demand for flexibility. Employees now expect options for remote work, flexible hours, and a greater degree of autonomy in their roles (Riggio, 2018). Companies that fail to offer these benefits risk losing out on top talent to more adaptable competitors. For instance, organizations like Google and Microsoft have successfully implemented flexible work policies, which have become key selling points in their talent acquisition strategies.

Another trend is the emphasis on company culture. Prospective employees are not just looking for a job; they are looking for a workplace where they can thrive and feel valued (Sull, 1999). This means that companies must cultivate a positive and inclusive culture to attract the best candidates. For example, Salesforce is renowned for its strong commitment to equality and social responsibility, which has helped it attract a diverse and talented workforce.

Case Studies: Successful Talent Acquisition Strategies

To illustrate the importance of adapting to these modern workforce trends, let us examine some case studies of companies that have successfully navigated the challenges of talent acquisition.

Case Study 1: Google

Google is a prime example of a company that has mastered the art of attracting and retaining top talent. The tech giant offers a range of benefits designed to appeal to the modern workforce, including comprehensive health insurance, generous parental leave, and flexible work options. Google's innovative office environments and commitment to employee well-being also play a significant role in its talent acquisition success (Riggio, 2018).

Moreover, Google places a strong emphasis on company culture. The company promotes a culture of innovation, collaboration, and inclusivity, which resonates with potential employees. This approach has helped Google maintain its reputation as one of the best places to work, consistently ranking high in employee satisfaction surveys.

Case Study 2: Microsoft

Microsoft has also adapted effectively to the changing dynamics of talent acquisition. Under the leadership of CEO Satya Nadella, Microsoft has embraced a growth mindset culture, encouraging employees to continuously learn and develop their skills. This cultural shift has been instrumental in attracting top talent who are eager to grow with the company (Dallas, 2015).

In addition to fostering a positive culture, Microsoft has implemented flexible work policies, recognizing the importance of work-life balance. The company's commitment to diversity and inclusion further enhances its appeal to a broad range of candidates. By aligning its talent acquisition strategies with modern workforce trends, Microsoft has successfully positioned itself as a desirable employer.

Case Studies: Unsuccessful Talent Acquisition Strategies

While some companies have thrived by adapting to modern workforce trends, others have struggled due to their inability to evolve. These case studies highlight the consequences of failing to address the changing dynamics of talent acquisition.

Case Study 1: General Electric (GE)

General Electric (GE) serves as a cautionary tale for companies that fail to adapt their talent acquisition strategies. In recent years, GE has faced significant challenges in attracting and retaining top talent. One key issue has been its rigid organizational structure, which has stifled innovation and limited flexibility (Benedict, 2007).

Furthermore, GE's focus on traditional incentives, such as competitive salaries and job security, has not resonated with younger generations who prioritize other factors. The company's lack of emphasis on creating a positive and inclusive culture has also hindered its ability to attract diverse talent. As a result, GE has struggled to compete with more adaptable companies in the talent market.

Case Study 2: Sears

Sears is another example of a company that failed to keep pace with the changing dynamics of talent acquisition. Once a retail giant, Sears faced a steady decline through the 1980s and 1990s, largely due to its inability to attract and retain top talent. The company's outdated business model and failure to embrace modern workforce trends contributed to its downfall and, ultimately, its demise(Sull, 1999).

Sears' reluctance to adopt flexible work policies and its lack of focus on employee well-being has made it an unattractive employer in today's competitive market. The company's failure to adapt its talent acquisition strategies has ultimately played a role in its decline.

Conclusion

The changing dynamics of talent acquisition present both challenges and opportunities for today's organizations. By understanding and adapting to modern workforce trends, companies can position themselves as desirable employers and attract the top talent needed to drive success. The case studies of Google and Microsoft illustrate the benefits of embracing flexibility, fostering a positive culture, and aligning with employee values. Conversely, the experiences of GE and Sears highlight the risks of failing to evolve. As the business environment continues to change, the ability to adapt will remain a critical factor in successful talent acquisition.

References

Benedict, A. (2007). 2007 change management survey report. Alexandria, VA: Society for Human Resource Management.

Dallas, H. J. (2015, October 22). Here are 4 ways leaders can deal with change. *Fortune*. Retrieved from http://fortune.com/2015/10/22/change-leaders-managers/

Manciagli, D. (2016, April 13). 4 biggest challenges facing business leaders today. *Biz Journals*. Retrieved from https://www.bizjournals.com/bizjournals/how-to/growth-strategies/2016/04/4-biggest-challenges-facing-business-leaders-today.html

Riggio, R. E. (2018, December 9). What is servant leadership and why does it matter? *Psychology Today*. Retrieved from https://www.psychologytoday.com/us/blog/cutting-edge-leadership/201812/what-is-servant-leadership-and-why-does-it-matter

Sull, D. (1999, July-August). Why good companies go bad. *Harvard Business Review*, 42–55. Retrieved from https://hbr.org/1999/07/why-good-companies-go-bad

CHAPTER 2

Compensation and Market Alignment

Personal Narrative: Compensation and Market Alignment

As the division head of multifamily construction at InnovateX, losing our top project manager, Mike, to a competitor offering a higher salary was a major blow. Mike's departure highlighted a critical issue: our compensation packages were not competitive with industry standards.

Realizing the urgency, I investigated our pay scales and found they hadn't been updated in years. The construction industry had evolved, and we were lagging behind in compensation. I took these findings to the executive team and pushed for a comprehensive market analysis.

The data confirmed our fears—we were significantly underpaying our staff. Working closely with HR and finance, we developed a strategy to adjust our salary bands and introduce performance bonuses. Implementing these changes required phased rollouts and transparent communication.

The results were immediate. Turnover decreased, and we attracted highly qualified candidates. Hiring a new project manager to replace Mike brought fresh expertise to our team, reinforcing the value of competitive compensation.

This experience taught me the importance of aligning pay with market standards. It's essential for retaining top talent and showing that we value their contributions, ultimately strengthening our division and enhancing our ability to deliver successful projects.

Introduction

As businesses navigate the complexities of the modern workforce, one of the most significant challenges they face is aligning their compensation structures with market realities. In a rapidly changing economic landscape, maintaining competitive compensation packages is essential for attracting and retaining top talent. This chapter explores the importance of understanding compensation trends, how companies can effectively align their compensation with the market, and practical guidelines to help organizations stay ahead in the talent acquisition game.

Understanding Compensation Trends

In the past, compensation primarily revolved around salary and basic benefits. However, today's employees have more complex and varied expectations. Modern compensation packages often include elements such as performance bonuses, stock options, flexible work arrangements, comprehensive health benefits, and professional development opportunities (Riggio, 2018). Understanding these trends is crucial for organizations looking to attract and retain top talent.

The Rise of Total Rewards

The concept of total rewards has gained significant traction in recent years. Total rewards encompass not only monetary compensation but also benefits, work-life balance, recognition, and career development opportunities (Manciagli, 2016). This holistic approach reflects the diverse priorities of today's workforce, where employees seek a balanced mix of financial and non-financial incentives.

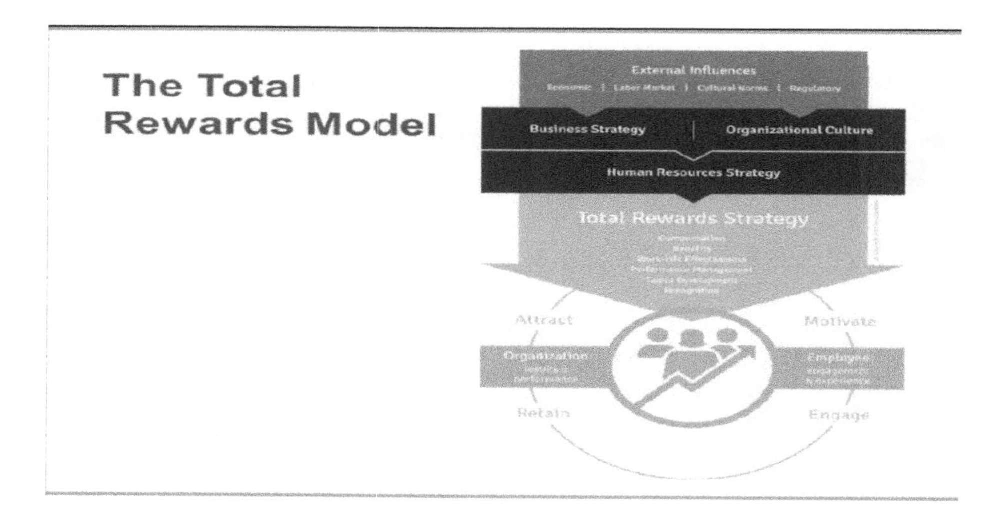

Source: WorldatWork. (2020). *Salary structure: How to develop and implement a compensation strategy*. WorldatWork Press.

Performance-Based Compensation

Performance-based compensation is another trend that has reshaped how companies reward their employees. This approach ties a portion of an employee's compensation to their performance, encouraging productivity and aligning individual goals with organizational objectives (Dallas, 2015). Companies like Salesforce and Amazon have successfully implemented performance-based compensation models, fostering a culture of accountability and excellence.

Equity and Stock Options

Equity and stock options have become a critical component of compensation packages, especially in the tech industry. Offering employees a stake in the company aligns their interests with the long-term success of the organization. Companies like Google, Microsoft, and many startups use stock options to attract top talent and incentivize employees to contribute to the company's growth (Sull, 1999).

Flexible Work Arrangements

Flexible work arrangements, including remote work and flexible hours, are increasingly valued by employees. The COVID-19 pandemic accelerated the adoption of these practices, proving that productivity can be maintained outside traditional office environments. Companies that offer flexibility as part of their compensation packages can attract a broader talent pool and improve employee satisfaction (Riggio, 2018).

Aligning Compensation with Market Changes

Staying competitive requires organizations to continually reassess and adjust their compensation strategies. This section outlines steps companies can take to ensure their compensation packages remain attractive in a dynamic market.

Conducting Market Research

Regular market research is essential to understanding how compensation trends evolve. This involves benchmarking against competitors, analyzing industry reports, and surveying employees to gauge their satisfaction and expectations. Tools like salary surveys and compensation consulting firms can provide valuable insights into current market standards (Manciagli, 2016).

Implementing Pay Audits

Pay audits are critical for ensuring equity and competitiveness in compensation structures. These audits help identify discrepancies and areas where the company may be lagging behind the market. Regular audits ensure that compensation remains fair and competitive, reducing the risk of losing top talent to competitors offering better packages (Dallas, 2015).

Adjusting Compensation Structures

Based on the findings from market research and pay audits, companies should be prepared to adjust their compensation structures. This might involve increasing salaries, enhancing benefits, or introducing new incentives such as performance bonuses or stock options. Flexibility and responsiveness are key to staying competitive (Riggio, 2018).

Communicating Changes Effectively

Transparent communication about compensation changes is crucial. Employees need to understand the rationale behind adjustments and how they benefit from these changes. Clear communication fosters trust and ensures employees feel valued and fairly compensated (Sull, 1999).

Practical Guidelines for Aligning Compensation

To effectively align compensation with market trends, organizations can follow several practical guidelines. These guidelines are designed to help companies create competitive, fair, and attractive compensation packages.

1. Develop a Comprehensive Compensation Philosophy

A well-defined compensation philosophy provides a framework for making consistent and equitable compensation decisions. This philosophy should reflect the company's values, business goals, and commitment to fairness and competitiveness (Riggio, 2018). For example, a tech company might emphasize innovation and reward employees with stock options and performance bonuses.

2. Customize Compensation Packages

One-size-fits-all compensation packages are less effective in today's diverse workforce. Customizing packages to meet the needs of different employee segments, such as remote workers, part-time employees, or those in high-demand roles, can enhance their attractiveness (Manciagli, 2016). For instance, offering flexible work arrangements can be a significant incentive for employees seeking better work-life balance.

3. Foster a Culture of Recognition and Rewards

Recognition programs that celebrate employee achievements and milestones can complement financial compensation. Regularly acknowledging employees' contributions boosts morale and reinforces a culture of appreciation (Dallas, 2015). Programs such as "Employee of the Month" or peer recognition platforms can be effective tools.

4. Leverage Technology for Compensation Management

Technology can streamline compensation management, making it easier to track, analyze, and adjust compensation structures. Compensation management software can help HR teams manage pay scales, performance bonuses, and equity distributions efficiently (Sull, 1999). These tools also provide data analytics to inform strategic decisions.

5. Engage Employees in Compensation Discussions

Involving employees in discussions about compensation can enhance transparency and trust. Regular feedback sessions and surveys can provide valuable insights into employee perceptions and expectations (Riggio, 2018). This participatory approach ensures that compensation strategies align with employee needs and market trends.

6. Monitor and Adapt to Legislative Changes

Legislation related to compensation and benefits is constantly evolving. Companies must stay informed about legal requirements to ensure compliance and avoid potential penalties. Keeping abreast of changes in labor laws, minimum wage standards, and tax regulations is essential (Manciagli, 2016).

7. Evaluate and Iterate Regularly

Compensation strategies should be dynamic and subject to regular evaluation. Continuous improvement ensures that compensation packages remain competitive and aligned with market changes (Dallas, 2015). Periodic reviews and adjustments based on market research and employee feedback are necessary to maintain effectiveness.

Case Studies of Effective Compensation Strategies

Examining real-world examples provides practical insights into how companies successfully align their compensation strategies with market trends.

Case Study 1: Salesforce

Salesforce, a global leader in customer relationship management (CRM), has garnered acclaim for its innovative compensation strategies. The company offers a comprehensive package that includes competitive salaries, performance-based bonuses, and stock options. Additionally, Salesforce emphasizes work-life balance, providing flexible work arrangements and generous parental leave policies (Riggio, 2018).

Salesforce's commitment to employee well-being extends beyond financial compensation. The company has robust wellness programs, including mental health support, fitness reimbursements, and wellness challenges. This holistic approach to compensation and benefits has helped Salesforce attract and retain top talent in a highly competitive market.

Case Study 2: Netflix

Netflix's unique compensation philosophy sets it apart in the entertainment industry. The company offers high salaries, often exceeding industry standards, and provides employees with the option to choose how much of their compensation they want in salary versus stock options. This flexibility allows employees to tailor their compensation to their individual needs and risk preferences (Dallas, 2015).

Netflix also emphasizes transparency in its compensation practices. The company publishes detailed guidelines on its approach to pay and performance, ensuring employees understand how their compensation is determined. This transparency fosters trust and aligns employee expectations with company policies.

Case Study 3: Patagonia

Patagonia, an outdoor apparel company, is renowned for its commitment to sustainability and employee well-being. The company offers competitive salaries and a range of benefits that reflect its values, including on-site childcare, flexible work hours, and generous time-off policies (Manciagli, 2016).

Patagonia's unique approach to compensation includes profit-sharing and annual bonuses tied to company performance. This ensures that employees share in the company's success and are motivated to contribute to its long-term goals. The company's focus on work-life balance and environmental stewardship has made it a desirable employer for those who share its values.

Case Study 4: Microsoft

Under CEO Satya Nadella's leadership, Microsoft has transformed its compensation strategies to align with a growth mindset culture. The company offers competitive salaries, performance bonuses, and stock options to attract top talent. Additionally, Microsoft has introduced flexible work policies, recognizing the importance of work-life balance (Riggio, 2018).

Microsoft's emphasis on continuous learning and development is reflected in its compensation packages. The company invests heavily in employee training and development programs, offering tuition reimbursement and access to a wide range of learning resources. This focus on professional growth has helped Microsoft attract and retain employees who are eager to advance their careers.

Conclusion

Aligning compensation with market changes is a critical component of effective talent acquisition and retention. By understanding modern compensation trends, conducting regular market research, and implementing practical guidelines, companies can create competitive and attractive compensation packages. The case studies of Salesforce, Netflix, Patagonia, and Microsoft demonstrate how innovative compensation strategies can help organizations stay ahead in the talent market.

As the business environment continues to evolve, companies must remain agile and responsive to changes in employee expectations and market dynamics. By fostering a culture of recognition, leveraging technology, and engaging employees in compensation discussions, organizations can ensure their compensation strategies remain effective and aligned with their overall goals.

Maintaining competitive compensation packages is not just about offering higher salaries; it is about creating a holistic approach that addresses the diverse needs and expectations of today's workforce. By doing so, companies can attract and retain the top talent needed to drive success in an ever-changing business landscape.

References

Benedict, A. (2007). 2007 change management survey report. Alexandria, VA: Society for Human Resource Management.

Dallas, H. J. (2015, October 22). Here are 4 ways leaders can deal with change. *Fortune*. Retrieved from http://fortune.com/2015/10/22/change-leaders-managers/

Manciagli, D. (2016, April 13). 4 biggest challenges facing business leaders today. *Biz Journals*. Retrieved from https://www.bizjournals.com/bizjournals/how-to/growth-strategies/2016/04/4-biggest-challenges-facing-business-leaders-today.html

Riggio, R. E. (2018, December 9). What is servant leadership and why does it matter? *Psychology Today*. Retrieved from https://www.psychologytoday.com/us/blog/cutting-edge-leadership/201812/what-is-servant-leadership-and-why-does-it-matter

Sull, D. (1999, July-August). Why good companies go bad. *Harvard Business Review*, 42–55. Retrieved from https://hbr.org/1999/07/why-good-companies-go-bad

CHAPTER 3

Organizational Flexibility and Employee Retention

Personal Narrative: Organizational Flexibility and Employee Retention

As the division head of multifamily construction at InnovateX, I quickly learned the importance of organizational flexibility for employee retention. When the pandemic hit, our rigid work schedules and processes were put to the test. Morale was low, and we faced the risk of losing valuable team members.

One particular moment stands out. Emily, one of our best project managers, approached me about the difficulty of balancing work with her family responsibilities during the crisis. She was considering leaving for a company that offered more flexible work options.

Realizing the gravity of the situation, I knew we needed to adapt quickly. I initiated a shift towards flexible work arrangements, allowing remote work and adjusting project timelines to accommodate our team's needs. We also introduced regular check-ins to support employees and address their concerns promptly.

These changes had an immediate positive impact. Emily decided to stay, and her productivity and job satisfaction improved. We noticed a significant boost in overall team morale and a reduction in turnover rates. By embracing flexibility, we not only retained key talent but also built a more resilient and motivated team.

This experience underscored the importance of organizational flexibility in retaining employees. By adapting to their needs and providing support, we created a more engaged and committed workforce, ready to tackle any challenges that came our way.

Introduction

The rapidly evolving business landscape demands that organizations remain agile and adaptable to survive and thrive. While attracting top talent is crucial, retaining these valuable employees is equally important. This chapter explores the role of organizational flexibility in employee retention, highlighting how companies can create adaptable structures that cater to the needs of their workforce. Through real-world examples and practical strategies, we will delve into the importance of fostering a flexible work environment to ensure long-term employee satisfaction and loyalty.

The Importance of Organizational Flexibility

In today's dynamic business environment, rigidity can be a company's downfall. Employees are increasingly seeking workplaces that offer flexibility, not just in terms of work hours but also in job roles, career paths, and work locations. Organizational flexibility is no longer a perk; it is a necessity for attracting and retaining top talent (Riggio, 2018).

Flexibility in Work Arrangements

Flexible work arrangements, including remote work, flexible hours, and compressed workweeks, have become highly valued by employees. These arrangements allow individuals to balance their professional and personal lives more effectively, leading to increased job satisfaction and reduced turnover rates (Manciagli, 2016).

Remote Work

The COVID-19 pandemic has accelerated the adoption of remote work. Companies that were quick to adapt to this shift have seen significant benefits in terms of employee retention. Remote work offers employees the flexibility to work from any location, reducing commute times and providing a better work-life balance. For example, tech companies like Twitter and Facebook have implemented permanent remote work policies, allowing employees to choose where they work best (Sull, 1999).

Flexible Hours

Flexible hours enable employees to adjust their work schedules to fit their personal needs. This flexibility can be particularly beneficial for working parents, caregivers, and those pursuing further education. Companies like Dell and Salesforce offer flexible work hours, allowing employees to start and finish their workday at times that suit them, as long as they meet their job requirements (Dallas, 2015).

Compressed Workweeks

Compressed workweeks allow employees to work longer hours over fewer days, such as four 10-hour days instead of five 8-hour days. This arrangement provides employees with additional days off, which can improve job satisfaction and reduce burnout. Companies like Basecamp and Unilever have experimented with compressed workweeks, reporting positive outcomes in terms of employee morale and productivity (Manciagli,

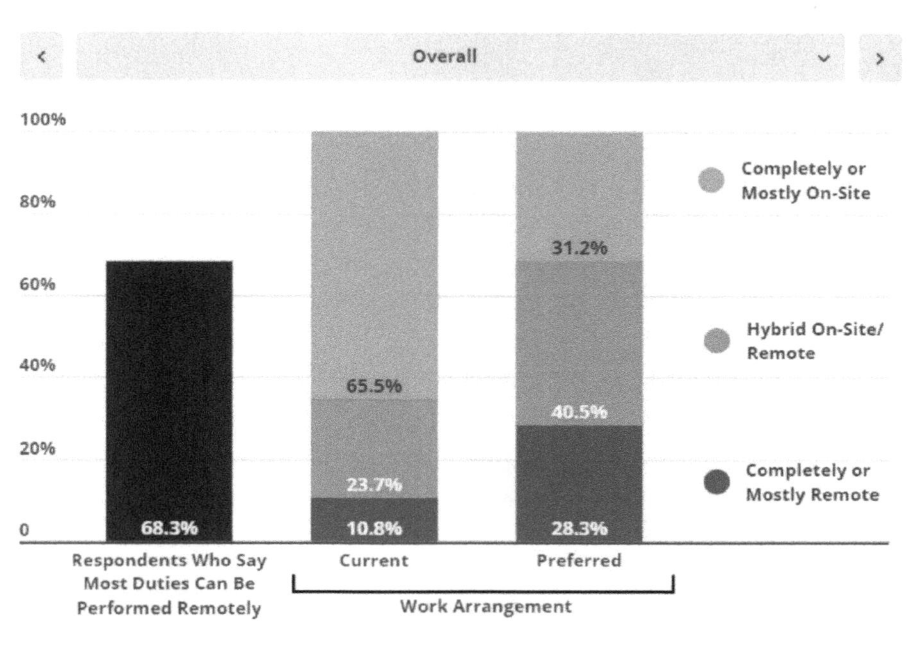

Source: Bichsel, J., Fuesting, M., Tubbs, D. & Schneider, J. (2023, September). *The CUPA-HR 2023 Higher Education Employee Retention Survey*. CUPA-HR.

Flexibility in Job Roles and Career Paths

Beyond work arrangements, organizational flexibility also encompasses job roles and career paths. Providing employees with opportunities to explore different roles and advance their careers within the organization can significantly enhance retention.

Job Rotation Programs

Job rotation programs allow employees to work in different departments or roles within the company. This not only helps employees develop a diverse skill set but also keeps them engaged and motivated. For example, IBM's job rotation program enables employees to experience various roles, fostering a culture of continuous learning and growth (Riggio, 2018).

Career Development Opportunities

Offering clear and diverse career development opportunities is crucial for retaining top talent. Employees are more likely to stay with a company if they see a path for advancement. Companies like Google and Microsoft provide extensive training and development programs, including leadership development courses, mentorship programs, and tuition reimbursement, ensuring employees have the resources they need to grow their careers (Sull, 1999).

Internal Mobility

Encouraging internal mobility allows employees to apply for open positions within the company. This can be particularly beneficial for retaining talent, as it provides employees with new challenges and opportunities without having to leave the organization. LinkedIn has a robust internal mobility program, allowing employees to explore different roles and departments, which has helped the company retain its top performers (Dallas, 2015).

Creating a Flexible Organizational Culture

Building a flexible organizational culture requires more than just implementing policies; it involves fostering an environment where flexibility is valued and supported at all levels.

Leadership Support

Leadership plays a crucial role in promoting organizational flexibility. Leaders must model flexible behaviors and support initiatives that enhance flexibility. This includes being open to remote work, flexible hours, and job rotation programs. Companies like Zappos have leaders who actively champion flexibility, creating a supportive environment for employees (Manciagli, 2016).

Employee Involvement

Involving employees in the decision-making process regarding flexibility can enhance buy-in and ensure that policies meet their needs. Regular surveys and feedback sessions can provide valuable insights into how flexibility can be improved. At Cisco, employee feedback is regularly solicited and used to shape flexible work policies, ensuring they are effective and beneficial (Riggio, 2018).

Technology and Infrastructure

Investing in technology and infrastructure that support flexibility is essential. This includes providing employees with the tools they need to work remotely, such as laptops, software, and secure internet access. Companies like Dropbox and Slack have invested heavily in technology to support their remote workforces, ensuring employees can stay connected and productive regardless of their location (Sull, 1999).

Case Studies: Successful Implementation of Flexibility

Examining how successful companies have implemented flexibility can provide valuable lessons for other organizations.

Case Study 1: Google

Google is renowned for its innovative approach to flexibility. The company offers a range of flexible work arrangements, including remote work options and flexible hours. Google's culture of flexibility is supported by robust technology infrastructure, allowing employees to work seamlessly from any location. The company's commitment to flexibility has resulted in high employee satisfaction and retention rates (Dallas, 2015).

Case Study 2: Unilever

Unilever has embraced flexibility through its "Agile Working" program, which allows employees to choose where and when they work. The program includes flexible hours, remote work options, and a focus on outcomes rather than hours worked. This approach has enabled Unilever to attract and retain top talent, with employees reporting improved work-life balance and job satisfaction (Manciagli, 2016).

Case Study 3: Salesforce

Salesforce's commitment to flexibility is evident in its comprehensive work-from-anywhere policy. The company provides employees with the tools and support they need to work remotely, including stipends for home office setups. Salesforce also offers flexible hours and promotes a culture of trust and autonomy. These initiatives have contributed to high levels of employee engagement and retention (Riggio, 2018).

Practical Strategies for Enhancing Organizational Flexibility

To effectively enhance organizational flexibility, companies can adopt several practical strategies. These strategies are designed to help organizations create a flexible work environment that meets the needs of their employees.

1. Develop a Flexibility Framework

A flexibility framework provides a structured approach to implementing flexible work arrangements. This framework should outline the types of flexibility offered, eligibility criteria, and guidelines for employees and managers. For example, a company might offer remote work options for certain roles while maintaining core hours for others (Dallas, 2015).

2. Train Managers on Flexibility

Managers play a crucial role in supporting organizational flexibility. Providing training on how to manage flexible teams, set clear expectations, and ensure accountability can help managers effectively implement flexible policies. At Microsoft, managers receive training on managing remote teams, which has helped the company successfully transition to a more flexible work environment (Manciagli, 2016).

3. Promote a Results-Oriented Culture

Shifting the focus from hours worked to results achieved can enhance organizational flexibility. This approach emphasizes productivity and outcomes, allowing employees to work in ways that best suit their needs. Companies like HubSpot have adopted a results-oriented culture, where employees are evaluated based on their contributions rather than their presence in the office (Riggio, 2018).

4. Provide the Necessary Tools and Resources

Ensuring employees have access to the tools and resources they need to work flexibly is essential. This includes providing laptops, collaboration software, and secure internet access. Investing in technology that supports remote work and flexible hours can enhance productivity and employee satisfaction. Dropbox has equipped its remote workforce with the necessary tools to stay connected and productive, resulting in a seamless transition to remote work (Sull, 1999).

5. Encourage Work-Life Balance

Promoting work-life balance is a key component of organizational flexibility. Encouraging employees to take breaks, use their vacation time, and disconnect after work hours can prevent burnout and improve overall well-being. Companies like Basecamp have implemented policies that support work-life balance, such as mandatory vacation time and restrictions on after-hours communication (Dallas, 2015).

6. Foster a Culture of Trust and Autonomy

Creating a culture of trust and autonomy is essential for successful organizational flexibility. Trusting employees to manage their own schedules and work independently can lead to increased job satisfaction and retention. At Zappos, a culture of trust and autonomy allows employees to work in ways that best suit their needs, resulting in high levels of engagement and loyalty (Manciagli, 2016).

Challenges and Solutions in Implementing Organizational Flexibility

While organizational flexibility offers numerous benefits, implementing it effectively can pose challenges. Understanding these challenges and finding solutions is crucial for creating a flexible work environment.

Challenge 1: Resistance to Change

Resistance to change is a common challenge when implementing organizational flexibility. Employees and managers may be accustomed to traditional work arrangements and reluctant to embrace new ways of working. To address this, companies can provide training and support to help employees transition to flexible work arrangements. Communicating the benefits of flexibility and involving employees in the decision-making process can also reduce resistance (Riggio, 2018).

Challenge 2: Maintaining Productivity and Accountability

Ensuring productivity and accountability in a flexible work environment can be challenging. Without clear guidelines and expectations, employees may struggle to manage their time effectively. To overcome this, companies can implement performance metrics and regular check-ins to monitor progress and provide feedback. Tools like project management software can help teams stay organized and accountable (Dallas, 2015).

Challenge 3: Technology and Security Concerns

Implementing organizational flexibility requires robust technology and security measures. Remote work, in particular, can pose cybersecurity risks if not properly managed. Companies must invest in secure communication tools, virtual private networks (VPNs), and cybersecurity training to protect sensitive information. Regular security audits and updates can ensure that technology infrastructure remains secure (Sull, 1999).

Challenge 4: Ensuring Inclusivity

Creating an inclusive flexible work environment is essential to ensure all employees benefit from flexibility. This includes considering the needs of different employee groups, such as remote workers, part-time employees, and those with caregiving responsibilities. Providing tailored support and resources can help ensure that flexibility is accessible to all employees (Manciagli, 2016).

Conclusion

Organizational flexibility is a critical component of employee retention in today's dynamic business environment. By offering flexible work arrangements, promoting internal mobility, and fostering a culture of trust and autonomy, companies can create a supportive and adaptable work environment that meets the needs of their employees. The case studies of Google, Unilever, Salesforce, and other successful companies demonstrate how effective flexibility strategies can enhance employee satisfaction and loyalty.

To implement organizational flexibility effectively, companies must develop a structured framework, provide training and support to managers, invest in the necessary tools and technology, and promote a results-oriented culture. By addressing challenges such as resistance to change, maintaining productivity, and ensuring inclusivity, organizations can create a flexible work environment that benefits both employees and the company as a whole.

As the business landscape continues to evolve, organizational flexibility will remain a key factor in attracting and retaining top talent. By embracing flexibility and continuously adapting to the needs of their workforce, companies can ensure long-term success and sustainability.

References

Benedict, A. (2007). 2007 change management survey report. Alexandria, VA: Society for Human Resource Management.

Dallas, H. J. (2015, October 22). Here are 4 ways leaders can deal with change. *Fortune*. Retrieved from http://fortune.com/2015/10/22/change-leaders-managers/

Manciagli, D. (2016, April 13). 4 biggest challenges facing business leaders today. *Biz Journals*. Retrieved from https://www.bizjournals.com/bizjournals/how-to/growth-strategies/2016/04/4-biggest-challenges-facing-business-leaders-today.html

Riggio, R. E. (2018, December 9). What is servant leadership and why does it matter? *Psychology Today*. Retrieved from https://www.psychologytoday.com/us/blog/cutting-edge-leadership/201812/what-is-servant-leadership-and-why-does-it-matter

Sull, D. (1999, July-August). Why good companies go bad. *Harvard Business Review*, 42–55. Retrieved from https://hbr.org/1999/07/why-good-companies-go-bad

CHAPTER 4

The Evolving Vision

Personal Narrative: The Evolving Vision

As the division head of multifamily construction at InnovateX, I've learned that having an evolving vision is crucial for success. When I first took on this role, our focus was primarily on completing projects on time and within budget. However, as the market changed, it became clear that we needed to adapt our vision to stay competitive.

One pivotal moment was during a quarterly review meeting. We were discussing a significant drop in client satisfaction. It became evident that our traditional approach wasn't meeting the new demands of our clients, who were looking for more sustainable and innovative solutions.

I knew we needed to pivot. I gathered my team and shared a new vision centered on sustainability and cutting-edge construction technologies. We set ambitious goals to reduce our carbon footprint and integrate smart home features into our projects.

This shift wasn't easy. It required retraining our staff, investing in new technologies, and redefining our project management processes. However, the commitment to this evolving vision paid off. We not only improved client satisfaction but also attracted new, environmentally-conscious clients and talented employees excited about our forward-thinking approach.

This experience taught me the power of an evolving vision. By continuously adapting and aligning our goals with market trends, we ensured our division's growth and long-term success.

Introduction

A company's vision is more than just a statement; it is the guiding star that drives strategic decisions and shapes the organizational culture. However, in a rapidly changing business environment, a static vision can become obsolete. This chapter explores the importance of evolving a company's vision to align with market dynamics and organizational growth. We will discuss how to create a dynamic vision, integrate it into the company's culture, and ensure it remains relevant over time. Through practical strategies and real-world examples, we will illustrate the critical role an evolving vision plays in achieving long-term success.

The Significance of a Dynamic Vision

A dynamic vision is essential for sustaining organizational relevance and competitiveness. It acts as a compass that guides the company through market shifts, technological advancements, and changing customer preferences (Dallas, 2015). A vision that evolves with the business environment ensures that the company remains aligned with its goals and can adapt to new opportunities and challenges.

Defining a Dynamic Vision

A dynamic vision is one that is adaptable and responsive to changes in the internal and external environment. Unlike static visions, which remain unchanged over time, dynamic visions are periodically reviewed and updated to reflect new realities. This approach helps organizations stay focused on their core mission while being flexible enough to pivot when necessary (Riggio, 2018).

Characteristics of a Dynamic Vision

1. **Future-Oriented:** A dynamic vision looks ahead and anticipates future trends and challenges.

2. **Flexible:** It allows for adjustments based on changes in the market, technology, and customer needs.

3. **Inclusive:** It involves input from various stakeholders, ensuring a comprehensive perspective.

4. **Clear and Concise:** It is easily understood and communicated throughout the organization.

5. **Actionable:** It provides a clear direction for strategic planning and decision-making.

The Benefits of a Dynamic Vision

A dynamic vision offers several benefits, including enhanced strategic alignment, improved adaptability, and increased employee engagement. By regularly updating the vision, companies can ensure that their strategic goals remain relevant and that employees are motivated to contribute to the organization's success (Manciagli, 2016).

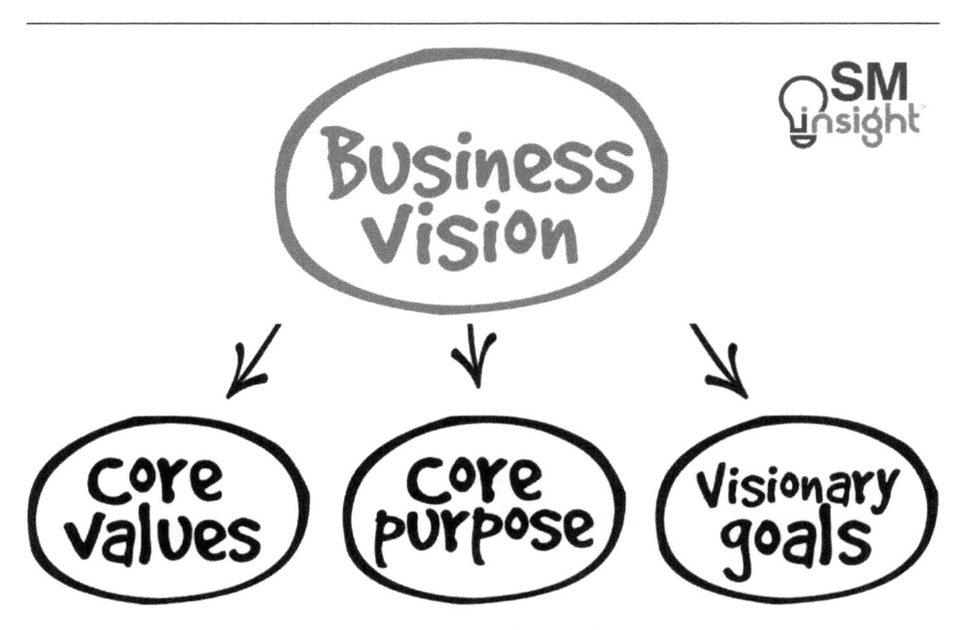

Source: Jurevicius, O. (2023, October 24). *Vision statement: The ultimate guide - SM insight.* Strategic Management Insight. https://strategicmanagementinsight.com/tools/vision-statement/

Creating a Dynamic Vision

Developing a dynamic vision requires a thoughtful and collaborative approach. This section outlines the steps involved in creating a vision that can evolve with the organization.

Step 1: Conduct a Comprehensive Environmental Scan

An environmental scan involves analyzing the internal and external factors that impact the organization. This includes assessing market trends, technological advancements, competitive landscape, and customer preferences. By understanding these factors, companies can identify potential opportunities and threats (Sull, 1999).

Step 2: Engage Stakeholders

Engaging stakeholders in the vision creation process ensures that the vision is comprehensive and inclusive. Stakeholders can include employees, customers, suppliers, investors, and community members. Conducting surveys, focus groups, and workshops can provide valuable insights and foster a sense of ownership among stakeholders (Riggio, 2018).

Step 3: Define Core Values and Purpose

The core values and purpose of the organization should be at the heart of the vision. These elements define what the company stands for and why it exists. Aligning the vision with the company's values and purpose ensures consistency and authenticity (Dallas, 2015).

Step 4: Draft the Vision Statement

The vision statement should be a clear and concise articulation of the company's aspirations. It should be inspiring and forward-looking, providing a sense of direction and purpose. The initial draft can be refined through feedback from stakeholders (Manciagli, 2016).

Step 5: Communicate the Vision

Effective communication is crucial for ensuring that the vision is understood and embraced by all members of the organization. This can be achieved through town hall meetings, internal newsletters, and digital platforms. Consistent messaging and storytelling can help reinforce the vision (Sull, 1999).

Step 6: Integrate the Vision into the Culture

Embedding the vision into the organizational culture involves aligning policies, practices, and behaviors with the vision. This includes integrating the vision into performance management systems, reward structures, and employee development programs (Riggio, 2018).

Step 7: Regularly Review and Update the Vision

A dynamic vision requires periodic review and updates. Establishing a review cycle, such as annually or biennially, allows the organization to assess the relevance of the vision and make necessary adjustments. This ensures that the vision remains aligned with the evolving business environment (Dallas, 2015).

Integrating the Vision into the Company Culture

For a vision to be effective, it must be deeply embedded into the organizational culture. This section explores strategies for integrating the vision into everyday practices and behaviors.

Aligning Leadership and Vision

Leadership plays a pivotal role in promoting and exemplifying the vision. Leaders must consistently communicate the vision and demonstrate behaviors that align with it. This includes making decisions that reflect the vision and holding themselves accountable to the same standards (Manciagli, 2016).

Developing a Vision-Aligned Strategy

A vision-aligned strategy ensures that all organizational initiatives support the vision. This involves setting strategic goals, allocating resources, and designing action plans that are consistent with the vision. Regularly reviewing strategic initiatives helps maintain alignment (Sull, 1999).

Building a Vision-Driven Workforce

A vision-driven workforce is motivated by a shared sense of purpose. This can be achieved through recruitment, onboarding, and training programs that emphasize the vision. Encouraging employees to contribute ideas and participate in vision-related initiatives fosters a sense of ownership (Riggio, 2018).

Recognizing and Rewarding Vision-Aligned Behaviors

Recognition and rewards are powerful tools for reinforcing the vision. Recognizing employees who exemplify the vision through their actions and contributions helps embed the vision into the organizational culture. This can include awards, promotions, and public acknowledgment (Dallas, 2015).

Case Studies: Successful Vision Integration

Examining real-world examples provides valuable insights into how companies successfully integrate their vision into their culture and operations.

Case Study 1: Tesla

Tesla's vision of accelerating the world's transition to sustainable energy is deeply embedded in its culture and operations. From its innovative electric vehicles to its solar energy solutions, Tesla's products and services reflect its commitment to sustainability. The company's leadership, led by CEO Elon Musk, consistently communicates and exemplifies the vision, inspiring employees and customers alike (Sull, 1999).

Case Study 2: Patagonia

Patagonia's vision of using business to inspire and implement solutions to the environmental crisis is central to its culture. The company's commitment to environmental sustainability is evident in its products, operations, and advocacy efforts. Patagonia encourages employees to participate in environmental initiatives and aligns its business practices with its vision, creating a strong sense of purpose and loyalty among its workforce (Dallas, 2015).

Case Study 3: Microsoft

Under the leadership of CEO Satya Nadella, Microsoft has embraced a vision of empowering every person and organization on the planet to achieve more. This vision has driven the company's transformation and innovation efforts. Microsoft's focus on cloud computing, artificial intelligence, and inclusive technology reflects its vision. The company's culture of continuous learning and growth aligns with its aspiration to empower others (Manciagli, 2016).

Practical Strategies for Keeping the Vision Relevant

Ensuring that a company's vision remains relevant over time requires ongoing effort and commitment. This section outlines practical strategies for maintaining the relevance of the vision.

1. Establish a Vision Review Committee

A vision review committee, comprising representatives from various departments and levels within the organization, can oversee the periodic review and update of the vision. This committee ensures diverse perspectives are considered and helps maintain alignment across the organization (Riggio, 2018).

2. Monitor Market and Industry Trends

Keeping abreast of market and industry trends is essential for maintaining a relevant vision. Regularly analyzing trends, competitive landscape, and customer preferences allows the organization to anticipate changes and adjust the vision accordingly (Sull, 1999).

3. Foster a Culture of Innovation

A culture of innovation encourages employees to think creatively and contribute ideas for evolving the vision. Innovation workshops, hackathons, and brainstorming sessions can generate fresh insights and drive continuous improvement (Dallas, 2015).

4. Engage Customers and Stakeholders

Engaging customers and stakeholders in the vision review process provides valuable external perspectives. Customer feedback, focus groups, and advisory panels can offer insights into how the vision resonates with key stakeholders and identify areas for refinement (Manciagli, 2016).

5. Communicate Changes Transparently

When updates to the vision are made, transparent communication is crucial. Explaining the reasons for changes and how they align with the company's goals and values helps maintain trust and buy-in from employees and stakeholders (Riggio, 2018).

6. Align Vision with Strategic Goals

Ensuring that the vision is integrated into the organization's strategic goals and objectives helps maintain alignment. Regularly reviewing and adjusting strategic plans based on the vision ensures that all initiatives support the long-term aspirations of the company (Sull, 1999).

Conclusion

An evolving vision is vital for navigating the complexities of today's business environment. By creating a dynamic vision that adapts to changes in the market, technology, and customer preferences, companies can maintain strategic alignment and drive long-term success. Integrating the vision into the organizational culture ensures that it guides daily operations and decision-making.

The case studies of Tesla, Patagonia, and Microsoft illustrate the power of a well-integrated and evolving vision. These companies have successfully embedded their visions into their cultures and operations, driving innovation and employee engagement.

Maintaining a relevant vision requires ongoing effort, including regular reviews, stakeholder engagement, and a commitment to innovation. By fostering a culture that supports continuous improvement and alignment with the vision, organizations can ensure they remain agile and competitive in a rapidly changing world.

References

Benedict, A. (2007). 2007 change management survey report. Alexandria, VA: Society for Human Resource Management.

Dallas, H. J. (2015, October 22). Here are 4 ways leaders can deal with change. *Fortune*. Retrieved from http://fortune.com/2015/10/22/change-leaders-managers/

Manciagli, D. (2016, April 13). 4 biggest challenges facing business leaders today. *Biz Journals*. Retrieved from https://www.bizjournals.com/bizjournals/how-to/growth-strategies/2016/04/4-biggest-challenges-facing-business-leaders-today.html

Riggio, R. E. (2018, December 9). What is servant leadership and why does it matter? *Psychology Today*. Retrieved from https://www.psychologytoday.com/us/blog/cutting-edge-leadership/201812/what-is-servant-leadership-and-why-does-it-matter

Sull, D. (1999, July-August). Why good companies go bad. *Harvard Business Review*, 42–55. Retrieved from https://hbr.org/1999/07/why-good-companies-go-bad

CHAPTER 5

Overcoming Organizational Inertia

Personal Narrative: Overcoming Organizational Inertia

As the division head of multifamily construction at InnovateX, I faced the daunting task of overcoming organizational inertia; or, in other words, “this is the way we do it”. Our processes were outdated, and resistance to change was strong. This became glaringly obvious during a critical project where delays and inefficiencies were costing us clients and revenue.

I realized we needed a drastic shift. During a heated project review meeting, I addressed the team about the necessity of adopting new technologies and streamlined workflows. The resistance was palpable, with many arguing that our traditional methods had always worked.

To break this inertia, I decided to lead by example. I implemented a pilot program using Building Information Modeling (BIM) on one of our smaller projects. I provided hands-on training and support to ensure the team felt confident using the new technology. The results were impressive—faster completion times, reduced errors, and higher client satisfaction.

Seeing the success of the pilot project, the team’s attitude began to shift. We gradually expanded the use of BIM across all projects, continually demonstrating its benefits. Over time, the resistance faded, and innovation became part of our culture.

This experience taught me that overcoming organizational inertia requires persistence, leading by example, and demonstrating tangible benefits. By pushing through the initial resistance, we transformed our operations, enhanced efficiency, and positioned our division for future success.

Introduction

Organizational inertia refers to the resistance to change within an organization. It manifests as a tendency to continue on a current trajectory, even when external conditions demand a shift. In a rapidly changing business environment, overcoming inertia is essential for survival and growth. This chapter delves into the causes of organizational inertia, its impact on business performance, and strategies to overcome it. By understanding and addressing the factors that contribute to inertia, organizations can become more agile and adaptable, positioning themselves for long-term success.

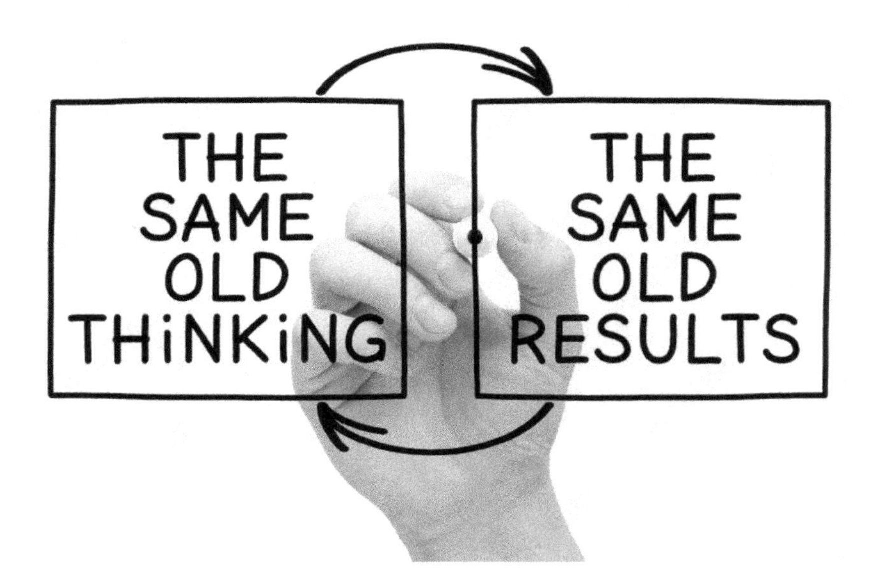

Understanding Organizational Inertia

Organizational inertia stems from a variety of factors, including established routines, structural rigidity, and cultural resistance. These elements create a sense of stability but can also hinder responsiveness to change (Riggio, 2018).

Causes of Organizational Inertia

1. **Established Routines and Processes**
   - Organizations develop routines and processes to ensure efficiency and consistency. Over time, these routines become deeply ingrained and difficult to change, even when they are no longer effective (Sull, 1999).
2. **Structural Rigidity**
   - Hierarchical structures and bureaucratic processes can create rigidity. Decision-making becomes slow and cumbersome, making it difficult to respond swiftly to market changes (Dallas, 2015).
3. **Cultural Resistance**
   - Organizational culture plays a significant role in inertia. A culture that values tradition and stability over innovation and change can resist new ideas and approaches (Manciagli, 2016).
4. **Risk Aversion**
   - Fear of failure and the potential risks associated with change can lead to a preference for maintaining the status quo. This risk aversion is often reinforced by a lack of incentives for innovation (Riggio, 2018).
5. **Resource Allocation**
   - Established organizations may have significant resources tied up in existing products, technologies, and markets. Reallocating these resources to new initiatives can be challenging and met with resistance (Sull, 1999).

Impact of Organizational Inertia

Organizational inertia can have profound negative effects on business performance. Companies that fail to adapt to changing conditions risk losing their competitive edge, experiencing declining market share, and ultimately facing obsolescence (Dallas, 2015).

1. **Loss of Competitive Advantage**
   - Inertia can prevent organizations from innovating and adapting to new market trends, leading to a loss of competitive advantage (Sull, 1999).
2. **Decreased Employee Morale**
   - A lack of responsiveness to change can result in frustration and disengagement among employees, particularly those who are eager to innovate and drive improvements (Manciagli, 2016).
3. **Declining Market Share**
   - Companies that fail to adapt may find themselves outpaced by more agile competitors, resulting in a loss of market share and revenue (Riggio, 2018).
4. **Operational Inefficiencies**
   - Rigid processes and structures can lead to operational inefficiencies, reducing productivity and increasing costs (Dallas, 2015).

Strategies to Overcome Organizational Inertia

Overcoming organizational inertia requires a multifaceted approach that addresses structural, cultural, and strategic elements. This section outlines practical strategies to help organizations become more agile and responsive to change.

1. Foster a Culture of Innovation

Cultivating a culture that values and rewards innovation is crucial for overcoming inertia. This involves encouraging creativity, experimentation, and a willingness to take risks (Manciagli, 2016).

Encourage Creative Thinking

Organizations can foster creative thinking by providing opportunities for brainstorming, collaboration, and cross-functional projects. Google's "20% time" policy, which allows employees to spend 20% of their time on projects of their choosing, is an example of how to encourage innovation (Riggio, 2018).

Reward Innovation

Recognizing and rewarding employees who contribute innovative ideas can reinforce a culture of innovation. This can include monetary incentives, promotions, and public acknowledgment. For instance, Salesforce offers bonuses and awards for employees who develop successful new ideas and projects (Dallas, 2015).

Provide Resources for Experimentation

Allocating resources for research and development (R&D) and innovation labs can encourage experimentation and risk-taking. These resources enable employees to explore new ideas without the pressure of immediate success. Companies like 3M and Procter & Gamble invest significantly in R&D to foster a culture of continuous innovation (Manciagli, 2016).

2. Streamline Decision-Making Processes

Simplifying decision-making processes can help organizations become more agile. This involves reducing bureaucratic red tape and empowering employees to make decisions (Sull, 1999).

Decentralize Decision-Making

Decentralizing decision-making authority allows teams and individuals to respond more quickly to changes and challenges. Companies like Amazon have decentralized decision-making, enabling faster responses to market trends. This approach encourages autonomy and accountability among employees (Riggio, 2018).

Implement Agile Methodologies

Agile methodologies, such as Scrum and Kanban, promote iterative development and continuous improvement. These approaches can help organizations respond more flexibly to changes. For example, software companies like Spotify use Agile frameworks to quickly adapt to user feedback and market demands (Dallas, 2015).

Reduce Bureaucracy

Eliminating unnecessary layers of approval and simplifying procedures can speed up decision-making. GE's "Work-Out" program, which encouraged employees to identify and eliminate bureaucratic inefficiencies, helped the company become more agile and responsive (Riggio, 2018).

3. Enhance Organizational Flexibility

Flexibility in structures and processes is key to overcoming inertia. This involves creating adaptable frameworks that can evolve with the organization's needs (Manciagli, 2016).

Adopt Flexible Structures

Matrix structures, where employees report to multiple managers, can enhance flexibility by breaking down silos and encouraging cross-functional collaboration. Cisco uses a matrix structure to foster innovation and responsiveness. This structure allows teams to be reconfigured quickly based on project needs (Riggio, 2018).

Implement Flexible Work Arrangements

Offering flexible work arrangements, such as remote work and flexible hours, can help organizations attract and retain top talent while enhancing agility. For instance, Dell's Connected Workplace program offers various flexible work options, which have improved employee satisfaction and productivity (Sull, 1999).

Embrace Cross-Functional Teams

Forming cross-functional teams can enhance collaboration and innovation. These teams bring together diverse perspectives and expertise, enabling more holistic and innovative solutions. For example, Apple's product development teams include members from engineering, design, and marketing, fostering creativity and efficiency (Dallas, 2015).

4. Invest in Change Management

Effective change management practices are essential for overcoming resistance and ensuring successful implementation of new initiatives (Dallas, 2015).

Develop a Change Management Plan

A comprehensive change management plan outlines the steps necessary to implement change, including communication strategies, training programs, and timelines. This plan helps ensure that all stakeholders are aligned and prepared for the transition (Riggio, 2018).

Engage Stakeholders

Involving stakeholders in the change process can help build support and reduce resistance. Regular updates, feedback sessions, and transparent communication are crucial for stakeholder engagement. For example, when Microsoft shifted to a cloud-first strategy, the company involved employees, customers, and partners in the transition, which helped gain widespread support (Manciagli, 2016).

Provide Training and Support

Training programs that equip employees with the skills and knowledge needed to adapt to new processes and technologies can reduce resistance to change. Offering ongoing support and resources helps employees feel more confident and capable during transitions. IBM's change management initiatives include extensive training and support, ensuring smooth adoption of new technologies (Sull, 1999).

5. Align Incentives with Strategic Goals

Aligning incentives with strategic goals ensures that employees are motivated to support change initiatives and organizational objectives (Sull, 1999).

Link Performance Metrics to Innovation

Incorporating innovation and adaptability into performance metrics can encourage employees to embrace change and contribute to organizational agility. For instance, Adobe's "Kickbox" program provides employees with a toolkit and funding to develop and test new ideas, rewarding successful innovations (Dallas, 2015).

Offer Long-Term Incentives

Long-term incentives, such as stock options and profit-sharing, can align employee interests with the organization's long-term success. These incentives encourage employees to focus on sustained performance and innovation. Companies like Google and Microsoft offer stock options to employees, fostering a sense of ownership and commitment (Riggio, 2018).

Recognize and Reward Change Champions

Identifying and rewarding employees who actively promote and support change initiatives can reinforce positive behaviors. Public recognition, bonuses, and career advancement opportunities can motivate others to follow suit. For example, at Zappos, employees who champion innovative projects and cultural initiatives are recognized and celebrated (Manciagli, 2016).

Case Studies: Overcoming Organizational Inertia

Real-world examples of companies that have successfully overcome organizational inertia provide valuable insights and inspiration.

Case Study 1: Microsoft

Microsoft's transformation under CEO Satya Nadella is a prime example of overcoming organizational inertia. Nadella's leadership focused on fostering a growth mindset, encouraging collaboration, and embracing new technologies. By decentralizing decision-making and promoting a culture of innovation, Microsoft successfully shifted from a stagnant tech giant to a leading player in cloud computing and AI (Dallas, 2015).

Case Study 2: General Electric (GE)

Under the leadership of Jack Welch, General Electric overcame significant organizational inertia by implementing a rigorous change management program. Welch introduced the "Work-Out" program, which encouraged employees at all levels to identify and eliminate bureaucratic inefficiencies. This initiative helped GE become more agile and competitive in the market (Riggio, 2018).

Case Study 3: Netflix

Netflix's transition from a DVD rental service to a leading streaming platform and content producer illustrates the importance of adaptability. CEO Reed Hastings emphasized a culture of freedom and responsibility, allowing teams to experiment and innovate. By continuously evolving its business model and investing in original content, Netflix overcame inertia and maintained its competitive edge (Sull, 1999).

Practical Strategies for Sustaining Agility

Sustaining organizational agility requires ongoing effort and commitment. This section outlines practical strategies to help organizations maintain flexibility and responsiveness over the long term.

1. Continuously Monitor the External Environment

Regularly monitoring the external environment helps organizations anticipate changes and adapt proactively (Dallas, 2015).

Conduct Market Research

Ongoing market research provides insights into industry trends, customer preferences, and competitive dynamics. This information can inform strategic decisions and help the organization stay ahead of the curve. Companies like Procter & Gamble use market research to identify emerging trends and adjust their strategies accordingly (Manciagli, 2016).

Engage with Industry Networks

Participating in industry networks and forums allows organizations to stay connected with peers and gain insights into emerging trends and best practices. For instance, IBM actively engages in industry consortia and technology forums to stay at the forefront of innovation (Riggio, 2018).

2. Foster a Learning Organization

A learning organization continuously seeks to improve by encouraging knowledge sharing, experimentation, and reflection (Sull, 1999).

Promote Continuous Learning

Offering training programs, workshops, and access to online learning resources can help employees develop new skills and stay updated on industry developments. Google's extensive training programs, including its Google Career Certificates, enable employees to acquire new competencies and advance their careers (Dallas, 2015).

Encourage Knowledge Sharing

Creating platforms for knowledge sharing, such as internal wikis, forums, and collaboration tools, can facilitate the exchange of ideas and best practices within the organization. At IBM, knowledge sharing is encouraged through various internal platforms, fostering a culture of continuous learning (Riggio, 2018).

3. Embrace Digital Transformation

Leveraging digital technologies can enhance organizational agility by improving efficiency, communication, and decision-making (Manciagli, 2016).

Invest in Digital Tools

Investing in digital tools, such as cloud computing, data analytics, and collaboration platforms, can streamline processes and enable more agile operations. Dropbox's use of cloud technology and collaboration tools has enhanced its ability to support remote work and improve productivity (Sull, 1999).

Implement Automation

Automation can reduce the burden of repetitive tasks, allowing employees to focus on more strategic and innovative activities. Companies like Amazon use automation in their warehouses and supply chains to improve efficiency and responsiveness (Dallas, 2015).

4. Build a Resilient Workforce

A resilient workforce is adaptable, resourceful, and capable of navigating challenges and uncertainties (Riggio, 2018).

Develop Resilience Training Programs

Training programs that focus on building resilience skills, such as stress management, problem-solving, and adaptability, can help employees cope with change. For example, Deloitte offers resilience training as part of its employee development programs (Manciagli, 2016).

Support Employee Well-being

Providing resources and support for employee well-being, such as mental health services, wellness programs, and work-life balance initiatives, can enhance resilience and productivity. Salesforce's comprehensive wellness programs, including mental health support and fitness reimbursements, contribute to a resilient workforce (Sull, 1999).

5. Maintain Strategic Flexibility

Strategic flexibility involves continuously reviewing and adjusting strategic plans to align with changing conditions (Dallas, 2015).

Regular Strategy Reviews

Conducting regular strategy reviews ensures that the organization's goals and initiatives remain aligned with the external environment. This can include quarterly or annual strategic planning sessions. Companies like Intel regularly review their strategies to stay competitive in the fast-evolving tech industry (Riggio, 2018).

Scenario Planning

Scenario planning involves exploring different future scenarios and developing strategies to address potential challenges and opportunities. This approach helps organizations prepare for uncertainty and adapt more effectively. Shell uses scenario planning to anticipate future energy trends and develop flexible strategies (Manciagli, 2016).

Conclusion

Overcoming organizational inertia is crucial for sustaining competitiveness and achieving long-term success in a rapidly changing business environment. By understanding the causes and impacts of inertia, organizations can implement strategies to enhance agility and responsiveness. Fostering a culture of innovation, streamlining decision-making processes, and investing in change management are key steps in overcoming inertia.

The case studies of Microsoft, General Electric, and Netflix demonstrate the power of adaptability and the benefits of overcoming organizational inertia. These companies have successfully transformed their operations and maintained their competitive edge by embracing change and fostering a culture of innovation.

Sustaining organizational agility requires ongoing effort, including continuous monitoring of the external environment, fostering a learning organization, embracing digital transformation, building a resilient workforce, and maintaining strategic flexibility. By committing to these strategies, organizations can overcome inertia and thrive in an ever-changing world.

References

Benedict, A. (2007). 2007 change management survey report. Alexandria, VA: Society for Human Resource Management.

Dallas, H. J. (2015, October 22). Here are 4 ways leaders can deal with change. *Fortune*. Retrieved from http://fortune.com/2015/10/22/change-leaders-managers/

Manciagli, D. (2016, April 13). 4 biggest challenges facing business leaders today. *Biz Journals*. Retrieved from https://www.bizjournals.com/bizjournals/how-to/growth-strategies/2016/04/4-biggest-challenges-facing-business-leaders-today.html

Riggio, R. E. (2018, December 9). What is servant leadership and why does it matter? *Psychology Today*. Retrieved from https://www.psychologytoday.com/us/blog/cutting-edge-leadership/201812/what-is-servant-leadership-and-why-does-it-matter

Sull, D. (1999, July-August). Why good companies go bad. *Harvard Business Review*, 42–55. Retrieved from https://hbr.org/1999/07/why-good-companies-go-bad

CHAPTER 6

Navigating Organizational Change

Personal Narrative: Navigating Organizational Change

As someone who has started the multifamily construction division in multiple companies, I understand the complexities of navigating organizational change. Each new division came with its unique set of challenges and resistance to change.

At my latest company, InnovateX, the need for change became clear when our initial projects faced significant delays and cost overruns. I knew we had to overhaul our processes to remain competitive. Drawing from past experiences, I decided to implement a comprehensive change strategy.

I began by communicating a clear vision for the division's future—emphasizing the need for agility, innovation, and efficiency. To build buy-in, I involved key stakeholders from the start, seeking their input and addressing their concerns. This collaborative approach helped to reduce resistance and foster a sense of ownership among the team.

Next, I introduced new project management software and lean construction principles to streamline operations. Training sessions were held to ensure everyone was comfortable with the new tools and methodologies. I also established regular feedback loops to monitor progress and make necessary adjustments.

The transition was challenging, with some initial pushback and a steep learning curve. However, by maintaining open communication and demonstrating the benefits of the changes, we gradually saw improvements. Project timelines shortened, costs decreased, and team morale improved.

This experience reinforced the importance of a clear vision, stakeholder involvement, and continuous communication in navigating organizational change. By staying committed to these principles, we successfully transformed our division and set a strong foundation for future growth.

Introduction

Change is inevitable in today's fast-paced business environment. Whether driven by technological advancements, market shifts, or internal growth, organizations must continuously adapt to remain competitive. However, navigating organizational change is a complex process that can be fraught with challenges. This chapter explores the principles and practices of effective change management, emphasizing the importance of leadership, communication, and employee engagement. By examining real-world examples and providing practical strategies, we aim to equip leaders with the tools needed to guide their organizations through successful change initiatives.

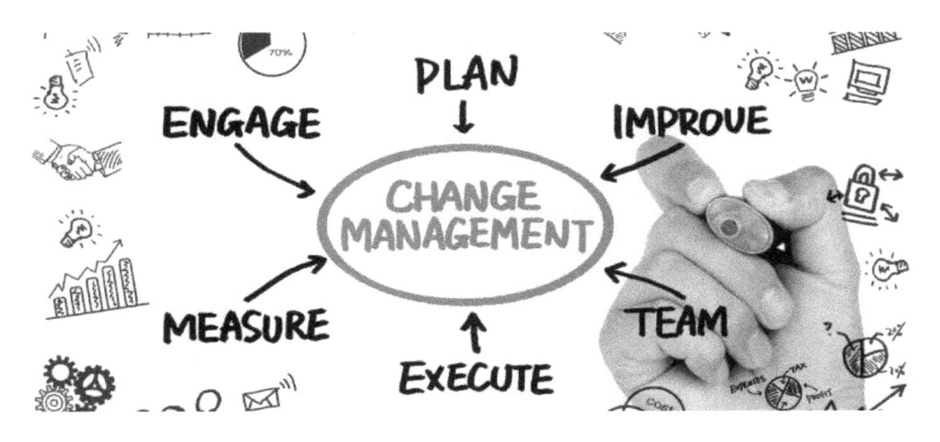

Source: Joseph, R. (2024, June 27). *Navigating organizational change effectively.* Navigating Organizational Change: Fostering a Culture of Adaptability. https://www.xcubelabs.com/blog/navigating-organizational-change-fostering-a-culture-of-adaptability/

The Nature of Organizational Change

Organizational change can take many forms, including restructuring, mergers and acquisitions, technological upgrades, cultural transformations, and strategic pivots. Each type of change presents unique challenges and requires tailored approaches to management (Riggio, 2018).

Types of Organizational Change

1. **Strategic Change**
   - Strategic change involves altering the organization's overall direction, such as entering new markets or changing the business model. This type of change often requires significant shifts in resources and capabilities (Dallas, 2015).
2. **Structural Change**
   - Structural change refers to modifications in the organization's hierarchy, reporting relationships, and operational processes. Examples include restructuring departments, creating new roles, or decentralizing decision-making (Manciagli, 2016).
3. **Technological Change**
   - Technological change encompasses the adoption of new technologies to improve efficiency, productivity, and innovation. Implementing new software, upgrading IT infrastructure, and automating processes are common examples (Sull, 1999).
4. **Cultural Change**
   - Cultural change aims to transform the organizational culture by reshaping values, norms, and behaviors. This type of change is often necessary to support other change initiatives and foster a more adaptable and innovative workforce (Riggio, 2018).
5. **People-Centric Change**
   - People-centric change focuses on the human aspect of the organization, such as improving employee engagement, diversity and inclusion initiatives, and leadership development programs (Dallas, 2015).

Challenges of Organizational Change

Organizational change is inherently challenging due to the complexity of human behavior and the interdependencies within organizations. Common challenges include resistance to change, communication barriers, resource constraints, and maintaining morale and productivity during transitions (Manciagli, 2016).

The Role of Leadership in Change Management

Effective leadership is critical to the success of any change initiative. Leaders must not only envision the future state of the organization but also inspire and guide their teams through the transition (Riggio, 2018).

Visionary Leadership

Visionary leaders articulate a compelling vision of the future that motivates and aligns the organization. They communicate the purpose and benefits of the change, helping employees understand why it is necessary and how it will impact the organization positively (Sull, 1999).

Transformational Leadership

Transformational leaders inspire and empower their teams to embrace change. They lead by example, demonstrating commitment and resilience, and provide support and resources to help employees navigate the transition (Dallas, 2015).

Adaptive Leadership

Adaptive leaders are flexible and responsive to emerging challenges and opportunities. They engage in continuous learning, seek feedback, and adjust their strategies as needed to ensure the success of the change initiative (Manciagli, 2016).

Engaging and Empowering Employees

Engaging employees in the change process is essential for overcoming resistance and ensuring successful implementation. Empowered employees are more likely to take ownership of the change and contribute positively to its outcomes (Riggio, 2018).

Effective Communication Strategies

Clear and consistent communication is a cornerstone of successful change management. It helps build trust, reduce uncertainty, and keep employees informed and engaged throughout the process (Dallas, 2015).

Developing a Communication Plan

A well-structured communication plan outlines the key messages, channels, and timelines for communicating the change initiative. It should address the needs and concerns of different stakeholder groups and provide regular updates on progress (Sull, 1999).

Key Components of a Communication Plan

1. **Objectives**
    - Define the goals of the communication plan, such as informing, engaging, and motivating employees.
2. **Audience Segmentation**
    - Identify the different stakeholder groups and tailor messages to their specific needs and concerns.
3. **Messaging**
    - Craft clear, consistent, and compelling messages that explain the purpose, benefits, and expected outcomes of the change.
4. **Channels**
    - Utilize a variety of communication channels, including emails, meetings, intranet, social media, and face-to-face interactions, to reach all stakeholders effectively.

5. **Timeline**

   - Establish a timeline for communication activities, including key milestones and regular updates (Riggio, 2018).

Encouraging two-way communication allows employees to provide feedback, ask questions, and express concerns. This helps build trust and ensures that leadership is aware of potential issues that may need to be addressed (Dallas, 2015).

Transparency and honesty are crucial for building trust during times of change. Leaders should be open about the challenges and uncertainties involved, as well as the steps being taken to address them. This approach fosters a culture of trust and credibility (Manciagli, 2016).

Employee Engagement and Involvement

Employee engagement is a critical factor in the success of any change initiative. Engaged employees are more likely to support the change, contribute ideas, and help overcome obstacles (Sull, 1999).

Building a Sense of Ownership

Involving employees in the planning and implementation of change initiatives can build a sense of ownership and commitment. This can be achieved through focus groups, task forces, and pilot programs that allow employees to contribute their insights and expertise (Riggio, 2018).

Recognizing and Rewarding Contributions

Recognizing and rewarding employees who actively support and contribute to the change initiative reinforces positive behaviors and encourages others to get involved. This can include public recognition, bonuses, and career advancement opportunities (Dallas, 2015).

Providing Support and Resources

Providing employees with the necessary support and resources, such as training programs, coaching, and access to information, can help them adapt to new processes and technologies. This reduces anxiety and builds confidence in their ability to navigate the change (Manciagli, 2016).

Fostering a Culture of Continuous Improvement

Encouraging a culture of continuous improvement helps sustain momentum and ensures that the organization remains adaptable and responsive to future changes. This involves regularly reviewing processes, soliciting feedback, and implementing incremental improvements (Sull, 1999).

Case Studies: Successful Change Management

Real-world examples of successful change management provide valuable insights and lessons for other organizations.

Case Study 1: Microsoft

Microsoft's transformation under CEO Satya Nadella is a prime example of successful change management. Nadella's leadership focused on fostering a growth mindset, encouraging collaboration, and embracing new technologies. By decentralizing decision-making and promoting a culture of innovation, Microsoft successfully shifted from a stagnant tech giant to a leading player in cloud computing and AI (Dallas, 2015).

Case Study 2: Starbucks

Starbucks faced significant challenges during the 2008 financial crisis, including declining sales and customer dissatisfaction. CEO Howard Schultz returned to lead the company through a turnaround, focusing on reconnecting with Starbucks' core values, improving customer experience, and innovating the product offering. Schultz's transparent communication, employee engagement initiatives, and emphasis on cultural change helped Starbucks regain its footing and achieve renewed success (Riggio, 2018).

Case Study 3: IBM

IBM's transformation from a hardware-centric company to a leader in cloud computing and AI required significant strategic and cultural change.

CEO Ginni Rometty led the company through this transition by focusing on innovation, investing in new technologies, and realigning the workforce. IBM's emphasis on continuous learning, employee engagement, and transparent communication helped the organization navigate the complex change process successfully (Manciagli, 2016).

Practical Strategies for Navigating Organizational Change

To effectively navigate organizational change, leaders can adopt several practical strategies. These strategies are designed to help organizations manage the complexities of change and achieve successful outcomes.

1. Develop a Comprehensive Change Management Plan

A comprehensive change management plan outlines the steps necessary to implement change, including communication strategies, training programs, and timelines. This plan helps ensure that all stakeholders are aligned and prepared for the transition (Riggio, 2018).

Key Elements of a Change Management Plan

- **Change Vision and Objectives:** Clearly define the vision and objectives of the change initiative, including the desired outcomes and benefits. The vision should be inspiring and clearly communicate the future state of the organization. Objectives should be specific, measurable, achievable, relevant, and time-bound (SMART).
- **Stakeholder Analysis:** Identify key stakeholders and assess their potential impact and influence on the change initiative. Map out all stakeholders, including employees, customers, suppliers, investors, and community members. Assess their interests, influence, and potential impact on the change initiative.
- **Change Implementation Strategy:** Outline the steps and actions required to implement the change, including timelines, milestones,

and responsibilities. Detail the specific steps required to achieve the change, including assigning roles and responsibilities, setting timelines, and establishing checkpoints for progress reviews.

- **Communication Plan:** Develop a communication plan to inform and engage stakeholders throughout the change process. Identify the key messages that need to be communicated, the appropriate channels for dissemination, and the frequency of updates. Ensure that communication is two-way, allowing for feedback and dialogue.
- **Training and Support:** Provide training and support to help employees adapt to new processes and technologies. Determine the training needs of different employee groups and develop tailored programs to address those needs. Provide ongoing support through coaching, mentoring, and access to resources.
- **Monitoring and Evaluation:** Establish metrics and mechanisms to monitor progress and evaluate the success of the change initiative. Define clear and measurable KPIs that align with the objectives of the change initiative. Regularly track and report on these metrics to monitor progress (Dallas, 2015).

2. Engage Stakeholders Early and Often

Involving stakeholders in the change process can help build support and reduce resistance. Regular updates, feedback sessions, and transparent communication are crucial for stakeholder engagement (Sull, 1999).

Strategies for Stakeholder Engagement

- **Stakeholder Mapping:** Identify and prioritize stakeholders based on their influence and impact on the change initiative. Create a visual representation of stakeholders, highlighting their interests, concerns, and the nature of their influence. This can help identify potential allies and detractors.
- **Engagement Activities:** Plan and execute engagement activities, such as workshops, focus groups, and town hall meetings, to gather

input and feedback from stakeholders. Use a variety of methods to engage stakeholders, ensuring that all voices are heard. Interactive workshops and focus groups can be particularly effective in fostering open dialogue.

- **Feedback Mechanisms:** Establish channels for stakeholders to provide feedback and express concerns, such as surveys, suggestion boxes, and online forums. Ensure that feedback channels are easily accessible and that stakeholders feel safe and encouraged to share their honest opinions. Regularly review and act on the feedback received.

- **Regular Updates:** Provide regular updates on the progress of the change initiative through newsletters, intranet posts, and meetings. Maintain a consistent communication schedule, providing updates on key milestones, successes, and challenges. Use a mix of formal and informal communication methods to keep stakeholders informed and engaged (Riggio, 2018).

3. Provide Training and Development Opportunities

Training and development programs equip employees with the skills and knowledge needed to adapt to new processes and technologies. Ongoing support and resources help employees feel more confident and capable during transitions (Manciagli, 2016).

Effective Training Strategies

- **Needs Assessment:** Conduct a needs assessment to identify the specific skills and knowledge required for the change initiative. Use surveys, interviews, and performance data to identify skill gaps and training needs. Engage employees in the assessment process to ensure that the training is relevant and targeted.

- **Customized Training Programs:** Develop customized training programs that address the identified needs and align with the change objectives. Develop training content that is specific to the roles and responsibilities of different employee groups. Use real-world scenarios and case studies to make the training practical and applicable.

- **Blended Learning:** Utilize a blended learning approach that combines in-person training, online courses, and hands-on workshops. Combine various learning methods to cater to different learning styles and preferences. Use online modules for theoretical knowledge and hands-on workshops for practical application.
- **Peer Learning:** Encourage peer learning and knowledge sharing through mentoring programs, team collaborations, and learning communities. Establish formal mentoring programs where experienced employees guide and support their peers. Encourage team-based projects and collaborative learning activities to foster a culture of continuous improvement.
- **Continuous Support:** Provide ongoing support and resources, such as coaching, job aids, and access to online learning platforms. Provide employees with access to resources such as online learning platforms, job aids, and coaching. Regularly update the training materials to reflect new developments and best practices (Sull, 1999).

4. Foster a Culture of Continuous Improvement

Encouraging a culture of continuous improvement helps sustain momentum and ensures that the organization remains adaptable and responsive to future changes. This involves regularly reviewing processes, soliciting feedback, and implementing incremental improvements (Riggio, 2018).

Strategies for Continuous Improvement

- **Process Reviews:** Conduct regular process reviews to identify areas for improvement and implement changes as needed. Schedule regular reviews of key processes, involving cross-functional teams to gain diverse perspectives. Use data and metrics to identify bottlenecks and inefficiencies.

- **Feedback Loops:** Establish feedback loops that allow employees to provide input and suggestions for improving processes and practices. Create formal and informal channels for employees to share their ideas and feedback. Act on the feedback promptly and communicate the changes made as a result.

- **Kaizen Events:** Organize Kaizen events, which are focused, short-term projects aimed at improving specific processes or areas of the organization. Plan and execute Kaizen events with clear objectives and timelines. Involve employees from different levels and departments to foster collaboration and innovation.

- **Lean and Six Sigma:** Implement Lean and Six Sigma methodologies to streamline processes, eliminate waste, and enhance quality. Train employees in Lean and Six Sigma principles and techniques. Use these methodologies to drive continuous improvement projects and track their impact on performance.

- **Recognition Programs:** Recognize and reward employees who contribute to continuous improvement initiatives, reinforcing the importance of ongoing enhancement. Develop a system for recognizing and rewarding employees who contribute to continuous improvement. Use a variety of rewards, such as bonuses, awards, and public acknowledgment, to reinforce positive behaviors (Dallas, 2015).

5. Monitor and Evaluate Change Progress

Monitoring and evaluating the progress of the change initiative is essential for ensuring its success. Regular assessments help identify areas for adjustment and improvement (Manciagli, 2016).

Effective Monitoring and Evaluation Strategies

- **Performance Metrics:** Establish key performance metrics to measure the success of the change initiative, such as productivity, employee engagement, and customer satisfaction. Define clear and measurable KPIs that align with the objectives of the change initiative. Regularly track and report on these metrics to monitor progress.

- **Progress Reviews:** Conduct regular progress reviews to assess the status of the change initiative and identify any issues or obstacles. Schedule regular progress reviews with key stakeholders to discuss the status of the change initiative. Use these reviews to identify and address any challenges or obstacles.
- **Surveys and Feedback:** Use surveys and feedback mechanisms to gather input from employees and stakeholders on the effectiveness of the change initiative. Develop and distribute surveys to gather feedback from employees and stakeholders. Use the feedback to assess the effectiveness of the change initiative and identify areas for improvement.
- **Benchmarking:** Compare the organization's performance against industry benchmarks and best practices to identify areas for improvement. Conduct benchmarking studies to compare the organization's performance against industry standards and best practices. Use the insights gained to identify opportunities for improvement.
- **Continuous Improvement:** Use the insights gained from monitoring and evaluation to make continuous improvements and adjustments to the change initiative. Create a culture of continuous improvement by regularly reviewing and adjusting the change initiative based on feedback and performance data. Encourage employees to contribute ideas for improvement and act on their suggestions (Sull, 1999).

Conclusion

Navigating organizational change is a complex but essential process for maintaining competitiveness and achieving long-term success. Effective change management requires visionary leadership, clear communication, employee engagement, and a commitment to continuous improvement. By developing comprehensive change management plans, engaging stakeholders, providing training and support, fostering a culture of continuous improvement, and monitoring progress, organizations can successfully navigate change and emerge stronger.

The case studies of Microsoft, Starbucks, and IBM demonstrate the power of effective change management and the benefits of embracing change. These organizations have successfully transformed their operations and maintained their competitive edge by fostering a culture of innovation, engaging employees, and implementing strategic changes.

By adopting the practical strategies outlined in this chapter, leaders can guide their organizations through the complexities of change and achieve successful outcomes. Embracing change and fostering a culture of adaptability will enable organizations to thrive in an ever-changing business environment.

References

Benedict, A. (2007). 2007 change management survey report. Alexandria, VA: Society for Human Resource Management.

Dallas, H. J. (2015, October 22). Here are 4 ways leaders can deal with change. *Fortune*. Retrieved from http://fortune.com/2015/10/22/change-leaders-managers/

Manciagli, D. (2016, April 13). 4 biggest challenges facing business leaders today. *Biz Journals*. Retrieved from https://www.bizjournals.com/bizjournals/how-to/growth-strategies/2016/04/4-biggest-challenges-facing-business-leaders-today.html

Riggio, R. E. (2018, December 9). What is servant leadership and why does it matter? *Psychology Today*. Retrieved from https://www.psychologytoday.com/us/blog/cutting-edge-leadership/201812/what-is-servant-leadership-and-why-does-it-matter

Sull, D. (1999, July-August). Why good companies go bad. *Harvard Business Review*, 42–55. Retrieved from https://hbr.org/1999/07/why-good-companies-go-bad

CHAPTER 7

The Role of Technology in Organizational Adaptation

Personal Narrative: The Role of Technology in Organizational Adaptation

Having started the multifamily construction division in multiple companies, I've seen firsthand how technology can drive organizational adaptation. At InnovateX, I recognized early on that we needed to embrace technology to stay ahead in the competitive construction industry.

Our traditional methods were causing inefficiencies and communication gaps, especially on the field. I decided to introduce Procore, a comprehensive construction management software, along with iPads for all our on-site managers. This was a significant change, but one I knew was necessary.

Implementing Procore allowed us to centralize project management, document sharing, and real-time updates. The use of iPads in the field meant our managers could access the latest plans, track progress, and report issues immediately, without having to return to the office. This integration vastly improved our workflow.

There was initial resistance, as some team members were uncomfortable with the new technology. To address this, I organized hands-on training sessions and provided ongoing support. Slowly, the team began to see the benefits. Issues were resolved faster, project timelines were more accurate, and overall efficiency improved.

One project stands out as a turning point. We were facing delays due to miscommunications about plan changes. With Procore and iPads, our field managers accessed updated plans instantly and coordinated seamlessly with the office. The project not only got back on track but was completed ahead of schedule.

This experience highlighted the transformative power of technology in organizational adaptation. By leveraging Procore and iPads, we improved communication, efficiency, and project outcomes, positioning our division for continued success in a rapidly evolving industry.

Introduction

In today's fast-paced and ever-evolving business environment, technology plays a crucial role in driving organizational adaptation and competitiveness. The integration of advanced technologies can enhance operational efficiency, foster innovation, and enable organizations to respond swiftly to market changes. This chapter explores the impact of technology on organizational adaptation, examines key technological trends, and provides strategies for leveraging technology to drive organizational change. By understanding and harnessing the power of technology, leaders can position their organizations for sustained success in an increasingly digital world.

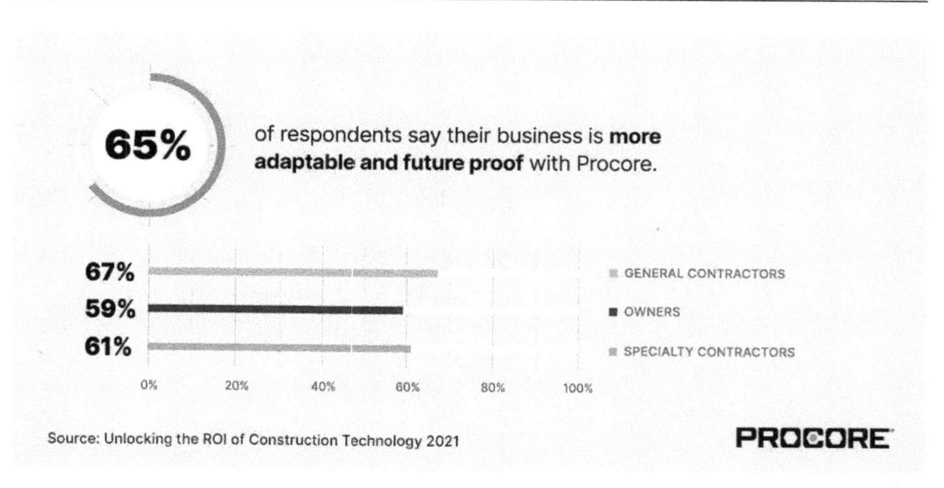

Source: Famularo, R. (2021, February 16). *How construction is using technology to improve performance*. Procore Corporate Blog. https://blog.procore.com/global-report-how-construction-is-using-technology-to-improve-performance/

The Impact of Technology on Organizational Adaptation

Technology has fundamentally transformed the way organizations operate, communicate, and compete. The ability to adapt to technological advancements is critical for maintaining a competitive edge and achieving long-term success (Riggio, 2018).

Enhancing Operational Efficiency

Technology can streamline processes, automate routine tasks, and improve productivity. For example, enterprise resource planning (ERP) systems integrate various business functions, such as finance, human resources, and supply chain management, into a single platform, enabling seamless data flow and real-time decision-making (Sull, 1999). By automating routine tasks, ERP systems free up employees to focus on more strategic activities, leading to higher productivity and efficiency.

Fostering Innovation

Advanced technologies, such as artificial intelligence (AI), machine learning, and big data analytics, enable organizations to innovate and develop new products and services. These technologies provide valuable insights, enhance predictive capabilities, and support data-driven decision-making, fostering a culture of innovation (Dallas, 2015). For example, AI can analyze customer data to identify unmet needs and preferences, leading to the development of new products that better meet market demands.

Enhancing Customer Experience

Technology has revolutionized customer interactions and expectations. Digital platforms, mobile applications, and social media enable organizations to engage with customers more effectively, provide personalized experiences, and respond promptly to customer needs. For example, customer relationship management (CRM) systems help organizations track customer interactions, analyze preferences, and tailor marketing strategies accordingly (Manciagli, 2016). This personalized approach not only improves customer satisfaction but also increases loyalty and retention.

Enabling Remote Work and Collaboration

The COVID-19 pandemic accelerated the adoption of remote work and collaboration technologies. Tools such as video conferencing, cloud computing, and project management software have enabled organizations to maintain productivity and collaboration despite physical distance. These technologies support flexible work arrangements, enhance work-life balance, and attract top talent (Riggio, 2018). For example, remote work tools like Slack and Zoom have become essential for maintaining communication and collaboration in distributed teams.

Key Technological Trends Driving Organizational Adaptation

Several technological trends are reshaping the business landscape and driving organizational adaptation. Understanding these trends and their implications can help leaders make informed decisions and leverage technology effectively.

1. Artificial Intelligence and Machine Learning

Artificial intelligence (AI) and machine learning (ML) are transforming industries by automating processes, enhancing decision-making, and enabling predictive analytics. AI-powered chatbots, for instance, can handle customer inquiries, reducing response times and improving customer satisfaction. Machine learning algorithms analyze vast amounts of data to identify patterns and provide actionable insights, supporting strategic decision-making (Sull, 1999).

AI in Customer Service

AI is revolutionizing customer service by enabling 24/7 support through chatbots and virtual assistants. These AI-driven tools can handle a wide range of customer queries, freeing up human agents to focus on more complex issues. For instance, companies like Sephora use AI-powered chatbots to assist customers with product recommendations and purchasing decisions, enhancing the overall customer experience (Dallas, 2015).

Predictive Analytics in Marketing

Machine learning algorithms enable predictive analytics, which can forecast customer behavior and optimize marketing strategies. Retailers like Amazon use predictive analytics to recommend products based on past purchases and browsing history, driving sales and improving customer satisfaction. This technology helps businesses anticipate customer needs and tailor their offerings accordingly (Manciagli, 2016).

2. Big Data and Analytics

The proliferation of data has given rise to big data and analytics, enabling organizations to gain deeper insights into customer behavior, market trends, and operational efficiency. By analyzing large datasets, organizations can identify opportunities for improvement, optimize processes, and develop targeted marketing strategies. For example, retailers use data analytics to forecast demand, manage inventory, and personalize customer experiences (Dallas, 2015).

Customer Insights and Personalization

Big data analytics allows businesses to gather and analyze vast amounts of customer data, providing insights into preferences, buying habits, and trends. This information can be used to create personalized marketing campaigns, improve product offerings, and enhance customer engagement. For instance, Netflix uses big data to analyze viewer preferences and recommend content, resulting in higher viewer satisfaction and retention (Riggio, 2018).

Operational Efficiency

Big data analytics also helps organizations improve operational efficiency by identifying inefficiencies and optimizing processes. Manufacturing companies use data analytics to monitor equipment performance, predict maintenance needs, and reduce downtime. This proactive approach to maintenance and operations enhances productivity and reduces costs (Manciagli, 2016).

3. Cloud Computing

Cloud computing has revolutionized the way organizations store, process, and access data. Cloud-based solutions offer scalability, flexibility, and cost-efficiency, allowing organizations to adapt quickly to changing needs. Cloud platforms enable remote work, facilitate collaboration, and support the deployment of new applications and services. Companies like Netflix leverage cloud computing to deliver content seamlessly to millions of users worldwide (Riggio, 2018).

Scalability and Flexibility

Cloud computing provides organizations with the ability to scale their IT resources up or down based on demand. This flexibility allows businesses to handle fluctuations in workload without investing in expensive hardware. For example, e-commerce platforms like Shopify use cloud computing to manage traffic spikes during peak shopping periods, ensuring a smooth customer experience (Sull, 1999).

Collaboration and Remote Work

Cloud-based collaboration tools, such as Google Workspace and Microsoft 365, enable teams to work together seamlessly from different locations. These tools support document sharing, real-time editing, and communication, making remote work more efficient and effective. During the COVID-19 pandemic, many organizations relied on cloud computing to maintain business continuity and support remote work arrangements (Dallas, 2015).

4. Internet of Things (IoT)

The Internet of Things (IoT) connects physical devices to the internet, enabling them to collect and exchange data. IoT technologies enhance operational efficiency, improve asset management, and enable real-time monitoring and control. For instance, smart factories use IoT sensors to monitor equipment performance, predict maintenance needs, and optimize production processes (Manciagli, 2016).

Smart Manufacturing

IoT is transforming manufacturing through the concept of smart factories, where connected devices and sensors collect real-time data on production processes. This data is used to optimize operations, reduce waste, and improve product quality. Companies like Siemens use IoT technologies to create digital twins of their manufacturing processes, enabling continuous monitoring and improvement (Riggio, 2018).

Supply Chain Optimization

IoT technologies also enhance supply chain management by providing real-time visibility into inventory levels, shipment status, and environmental conditions. Retailers like Walmart use IoT sensors to track the movement of goods through their supply chain, ensuring timely deliveries and reducing losses due to spoilage or theft (Sull, 1999).

5. Blockchain Technology

Blockchain technology provides a secure and transparent way to record transactions and track assets. It has applications in various industries, including finance, supply chain management, and healthcare. Blockchain enhances security, reduces fraud, and improves traceability. For example, supply chain companies use blockchain to track the provenance of goods, ensuring transparency and trust (Sull, 1999).

Financial Services

Blockchain is revolutionizing financial services by enabling secure and transparent transactions. Cryptocurrencies like Bitcoin and Ethereum use blockchain to facilitate peer-to-peer transactions without the need for intermediaries. Financial institutions are also exploring blockchain for cross-border payments, reducing transaction times and costs (Dallas, 2015).

Supply Chain Transparency

Blockchain provides end-to-end transparency in supply chains, allowing stakeholders to track the origin and movement of goods. This transparency helps combat fraud, ensure product authenticity, and improve accountability. For instance, IBM's Food Trust blockchain platform enables retailers and suppliers to trace the journey of food products from farm to table, ensuring food safety and quality (Manciagli, 2016).

Strategies for Leveraging Technology to Drive Organizational Change

To effectively leverage technology for organizational adaptation, leaders must develop and implement strategic approaches. This section outlines key strategies for harnessing technology to drive change and achieve business objectives.

1. Align Technology with Business Goals

Aligning technology initiatives with business goals ensures that technology investments support the organization's strategic objectives. Leaders should involve key stakeholders in the planning process, identify technology needs, and prioritize projects that deliver the most value. For example, a retail company aiming to enhance customer experience might invest in AI-powered chatbots and data analytics to personalize interactions and optimize marketing campaigns (Dallas, 2015).

Collaborative Planning

Involve cross-functional teams in the technology planning process to ensure that initiatives align with business objectives and address the needs of different departments. Regularly review and update the technology strategy to reflect changing business priorities and market conditions (Riggio, 2018).

Prioritization and ROI

Prioritize technology projects based on their potential return on investment (ROI) and alignment with strategic goals. Develop a clear business case for each initiative, outlining the expected benefits, costs, and risks. Monitor and evaluate the performance of technology investments to ensure they deliver the desired outcomes (Sull, 1999).

2. Foster a Culture of Innovation

Creating a culture of innovation encourages employees to embrace new technologies and explore creative solutions. Leaders should promote experimentation, provide resources for innovation, and recognize and reward innovative ideas. Google's "20% time" policy, which allows employees to spend 20% of their time on passion projects, fosters a culture of innovation and has led to the development of successful products like Gmail and Google News (Riggio, 2018).

Encouraging Experimentation

Provide employees with the freedom and resources to experiment with new ideas and technologies. Create innovation labs, hackathons, and pilot programs to encourage creative problem-solving and rapid prototyping. Celebrate successes and learn from failures to foster a culture of continuous improvement (Dallas, 2015).

Recognition and Rewards

Recognize and reward employees who contribute innovative ideas and solutions. Implement incentive programs, such as bonuses, awards, and public recognition, to motivate employees and reinforce the importance of innovation. Highlight success stories and share best practices across the organization to inspire others (Manciagli, 2016).

3. Invest in Digital Transformation

Digital transformation involves the integration of digital technologies into all aspects of the business, fundamentally changing how the organization operates and delivers value. This requires a comprehensive strategy, including upgrading legacy systems, adopting new technologies, and developing digital capabilities. Companies like General Electric (GE) have undergone digital transformations, leveraging IoT and data analytics to enhance operational efficiency and drive innovation (Sull, 1999).

Comprehensive Strategy

Develop a comprehensive digital transformation strategy that aligns with the organization's vision and goals. Assess the current state of digital capabilities, identify gaps, and prioritize initiatives that will drive the most significant impact. Engage stakeholders at all levels to ensure buy-in and support for the transformation (Riggio, 2018).

Legacy System Upgrades

Upgrade or replace legacy systems with modern, scalable, and flexible solutions that support digital initiatives. Consider cloud-based platforms, AI, and data analytics tools to enhance efficiency and enable real-time decision-making. Ensure that new systems are interoperable and can integrate seamlessly with existing technologies (Dallas, 2015).

Developing Digital Capabilities

Invest in building digital capabilities within the workforce. Provide training and development programs to equip employees with the skills needed to leverage new technologies effectively. Foster a culture of continuous learning and innovation to keep pace with technological advancements (Manciagli, 2016).

4. Enhance Data Management and Security

Effective data management and security are critical for leveraging technology and protecting sensitive information. Organizations should implement robust data governance frameworks, invest in cybersecurity measures, and comply with data protection regulations. For example, financial institutions must adhere to stringent data privacy laws and implement advanced encryption and access controls to safeguard customer data (Riggio, 2018).

Data Governance

Implement a data governance framework to ensure the accuracy, consistency, and security of data across the organization. Establish data ownership, define data standards, and implement data quality controls. Regularly review and update data governance policies to address emerging risks and regulatory requirements (Sull, 1999).

Cybersecurity Measures

Invest in advanced cybersecurity measures to protect against data breaches, cyberattacks, and other threats. Implement multi-factor authentication, encryption, and access controls to safeguard sensitive information. Conduct regular security audits and vulnerability assessments to identify and address potential risks (Dallas, 2015).

Compliance and Privacy

Ensure compliance with data protection regulations, such as the General Data Protection Regulation (GDPR) and the California Consumer Privacy Act (CCPA). Develop and enforce data privacy policies to protect customer information and build trust. Provide training and resources to employees to ensure they understand and adhere to data privacy requirements (Manciagli, 2016).

5. Build Digital Skills and Capabilities

Developing digital skills and capabilities within the workforce is essential for successful technology adoption. Organizations should provide training and development programs to equip employees with the necessary skills to use new technologies effectively. Companies like IBM offer extensive training programs in AI, cloud computing, and data analytics, ensuring their workforce is prepared for the digital future (Riggio, 2018).

Training and Development Programs

Implement comprehensive training and development programs to build digital skills and capabilities. Offer a mix of in-person training, online courses, and hands-on workshops to cater to different learning styles. Provide opportunities for continuous learning and professional development to keep employees up-to-date with technological advancements (Dallas, 2015).

Talent Acquisition and Retention

Attract and retain top digital talent by offering competitive compensation, career development opportunities, and a positive work environment. Develop partnerships with educational institutions to create talent pipelines and support internship and apprenticeship programs. Recognize and reward employees who demonstrate digital expertise and contribute to technology initiatives (Manciagli, 2016).

6. Foster Collaboration and Cross-Functional Teams

Technology-driven change often requires collaboration across different functions and departments. Cross-functional teams bring diverse perspectives and expertise, enabling more holistic and innovative solutions. Leaders should create opportunities for collaboration, such as innovation labs, hackathons, and cross-departmental projects. For instance, Apple's product development teams include members from engineering, design, and marketing, fostering creativity and efficiency (Dallas, 2015).

Creating Collaborative Environments

Design physical and virtual workspaces that promote collaboration and knowledge sharing. Use collaborative tools and platforms, such as Slack, Microsoft Teams, and Asana, to facilitate communication and project management. Encourage open communication and transparency to build trust and foster a collaborative culture (Riggio, 2018).

Cross-Functional Teams

Form cross-functional teams to address complex challenges and drive innovation. Include members from different departments and levels to ensure diverse perspectives and expertise. Provide training and resources to support effective teamwork and collaboration. Recognize and celebrate team achievements to reinforce the value of collaboration (Sull, 1999).

7. Continuously Monitor and Adapt

The rapid pace of technological change requires organizations to continuously monitor the technology landscape and adapt accordingly. Leaders should stay informed about emerging technologies, assess their potential impact, and adjust strategies as needed. This proactive approach ensures that the organization remains agile and responsive to new opportunities and challenges. Companies like Amazon constantly innovate and adapt their technology strategies to maintain their competitive edge (Sull, 1999).

Technology Scanning

Regularly scan the technology landscape to identify emerging trends and innovations. Subscribe to industry publications, attend conferences, and participate in professional networks to stay informed about the latest developments. Use this information to inform strategic planning and decision-making (Dallas, 2015).

Agile Adaptation

Adopt agile methodologies to enable rapid adaptation to changing conditions. Use iterative development and continuous feedback to refine technology initiatives and respond to new challenges. Implement pilot programs and phased rollouts to test and validate new technologies before full-scale deployment (Manciagli, 2016).

Performance Monitoring

Continuously monitor the performance of technology initiatives to ensure they deliver the desired outcomes. Use key performance indicators (KPIs) to track progress and identify areas for improvement. Regularly review and adjust strategies to align with evolving business goals and market conditions (Riggio, 2018).

Conclusion

Technology plays a pivotal role in driving organizational adaptation and competitiveness. By understanding and leveraging key technological trends, organizations can enhance operational efficiency, foster innovation, and respond effectively to market changes. Successful technology adoption requires strategic alignment, a culture of innovation, robust data management, and continuous learning.

The case studies of Netflix, Amazon, and Tesla illustrate the transformative power of technology-driven adaptation. These organizations have leveraged advanced technologies to revolutionize their industries, enhance customer experiences, and achieve sustained success.

By adopting the strategies outlined in this chapter, leaders can harness the power of technology to drive organizational change and achieve long-term success. Embracing technology and fostering a culture of adaptability will enable organizations to thrive in an increasingly digital world.

References

Benedict, A. (2007). 2007 change management survey report. Alexandria, VA: Society for Human Resource Management.

Dallas, H. J. (2015, October 22). Here are 4 ways leaders can deal with change. *Fortune*. Retrieved from http://fortune.com/2015/10/22/change-leaders-managers/

Manciagli, D. (2016, April 13). 4 biggest challenges facing business leaders today. *Biz Journals*. Retrieved from https://www.bizjournals.com/bizjournals/how-to/growth-strategies/2016/04/4-biggest-challenges-facing-business-leaders-today.html

Riggio, R. E. (2018, December 9). What is servant leadership and why does it matter? *Psychology Today*. Retrieved from https://www.psychologytoday.com/us/blog/cutting-edge-leadership/201812/what-is-servant-leadership-and-why-does-it-matter

Sull, D. (1999, July-August). Why good companies go bad. *Harvard Business Review*, 42–55. Retrieved from https://hbr.org/1999/07/why-good-companies-go-bad

CHAPTER 8

Cultivating a Resilient Organizational Culture

Personal Narrative: Cultivating a Resilient Organizational Culture

After almost three decades in the multi-family construction industry, working with multiple companies, I've experienced the cyclical nature of our industry firsthand. Booms and busts are inevitable, and cultivating a resilient organizational culture is crucial for weathering these cycles.

At InnovateX, we faced a significant downturn not long after launching our new division. Projects were being postponed, and the uncertainty took a toll on team morale. Drawing from past experiences, I knew that fostering resilience was key to navigating these tough times.

I began by promoting open communication, ensuring everyone was informed about the challenges and our strategy to overcome them. Transparency helped build trust and kept the team focused. I also emphasized the importance of flexibility and adaptability, encouraging creative problem-solving and new approaches to maintaining productivity.

We implemented regular training sessions to upskill our team, preparing them for diverse roles and responsibilities. This not only enhanced their capabilities but also kept them engaged and motivated. During slower periods, we focused on internal projects and process improvements, turning downtime into an opportunity for growth.

One initiative that stood out was our mentoring program. Pairing less experienced employees with seasoned veterans helped transfer knowledge and build a supportive network within the team. This sense of camaraderie and shared purpose strengthened our collective resilience.

As the market began to recover, our team was well-prepared to seize new opportunities. The proactive steps we took during the downturn paid off, as we quickly ramped up operations and secured new projects. Our resilience enabled us to not just survive but thrive.

This experience reinforced the importance of cultivating a resilient organizational culture. By fostering open communication, flexibility, continuous learning, and strong support networks, we built a team capable of enduring industry cycles and emerging stronger.

Introduction

In an era characterized by rapid change and uncertainty, cultivating a resilient organizational culture is essential for long-term success. A resilient culture enables organizations to withstand challenges, adapt to shifting conditions, and seize new opportunities. This chapter explores the key components of organizational resilience, examines strategies for fostering resilience, and highlights the role of leadership in building a resilient culture. By understanding and implementing these strategies, leaders can create an environment that not only survives but thrives amidst adversity.

The Importance of Organizational Resilience

Organizational resilience refers to the ability of an organization to anticipate, prepare for, respond to, and recover from disruptions and challenges. A resilient organization can maintain core functions and quickly adapt to new circumstances, ensuring continuity and sustained performance (Riggio, 2018).

Adaptability and Agility

Adaptability and agility are core components of organizational resilience. Adaptability refers to the organization's capacity to adjust its strategies, structures, and processes in response to changing conditions. Agility, on the other hand, is the ability to move quickly and efficiently in response to new opportunities and threats. Organizations that are both adaptable and agile can pivot as needed, maintaining relevance and competitiveness in dynamic environments (Sull, 1999).

Employee Engagement and Well-being

Employee engagement and well-being are critical to organizational resilience. Engaged employees are more committed, motivated, and willing to go the extra mile during times of crisis. Additionally, organizations that prioritize employee well-being—by providing support, resources, and a positive work environment—can foster a workforce that is better equipped to handle stress and uncertainty (Dallas, 2015).

Strong Leadership

Effective leadership is paramount in building organizational resilience. Leaders set the tone for the organization, shaping its culture and guiding its response to challenges. Resilient leaders demonstrate qualities such as vision, adaptability, empathy, and decisiveness, inspiring confidence and stability in their teams (Manciagli, 2016).

Continuous Learning and Innovation

A culture of continuous learning and innovation enhances organizational resilience by encouraging employees to develop new skills, experiment with new ideas, and embrace change. Organizations that invest in learning and development can better navigate disruptions and capitalize on emerging opportunities (Riggio, 2018).

Key Components of Organizational Resilience

Understanding the key components of organizational resilience is the first step in cultivating a resilient culture. These components provide a foundation for building and sustaining resilience in the face of challenges.

1. Vision and Purpose

A clear and compelling vision and purpose provide direction and motivation for the organization. During times of uncertainty, a strong sense of purpose helps align efforts and maintain focus on long-term goals. Leaders should articulate a vision that inspires and unites the organization, reinforcing the importance of resilience (Sull, 1999).

Defining Vision and Purpose

A well-defined vision and purpose should reflect the organization's core values and long-term aspirations. It should be communicated clearly and consistently to all stakeholders, serving as a guiding star during turbulent times. For example, Patagonia's vision of environmental stewardship and sustainability guides its business decisions and inspires its employees to work toward a greater good (Dallas, 2015).

2. Leadership Commitment

Leadership commitment to resilience is crucial for fostering a resilient culture. Leaders must model resilient behaviors, such as adaptability, perseverance, and a positive attitude. They should also prioritize resilience in strategic planning and decision-making, ensuring that the organization is prepared to face challenges (Manciagli, 2016).

Demonstrating Resilient Leadership

Resilient leaders demonstrate a commitment to resilience through their actions and decisions. They remain calm under pressure, communicate transparently, and make informed decisions based on the best available information. By exemplifying resilience, leaders can inspire their teams to adopt similar behaviors (Riggio, 2018).

3. Robust Communication

Effective communication is essential for building and maintaining resilience. Clear, transparent, and frequent communication helps ensure that employees are informed, engaged, and aligned with the organization's goals. During times of crisis, communication becomes even more critical, providing guidance, reassurance, and a sense of stability (Sull, 1999).

Strategies for Effective Communication

Develop a comprehensive communication plan that includes regular updates, two-way feedback mechanisms, and multiple channels for disseminating information. Encourage open dialogue and active listening, ensuring that employees feel heard and valued. For instance, during the

COVID-19 pandemic, companies like Microsoft held regular virtual town halls to keep employees informed and connected (Dallas, 2015).

4. Employee Empowerment

Empowering employees to take initiative and make decisions enhances organizational resilience. When employees feel trusted and capable, they are more likely to respond effectively to challenges and contribute to the organization's adaptability. Empowerment fosters a sense of ownership and accountability, driving proactive problem-solving (Manciagli, 2016).

Creating an Empowering Environment

Foster an empowering environment by providing employees with the resources, training, and support they need to succeed. Encourage autonomy and decision-making at all levels, and recognize and reward employees for their contributions. Google's culture of empowerment and autonomy has led to significant innovations and resilience within the organization (Riggio, 2018).

5. Flexible and Inclusive Work Environment

A flexible and inclusive work environment supports resilience by accommodating diverse needs and promoting work-life balance. Flexible work arrangements, such as remote work and flexible hours, enable employees to manage personal and professional responsibilities more effectively. Inclusivity ensures that all employees feel valued and supported, regardless of their background or circumstances (Sull, 1999).

Implementing Flexibility and Inclusivity

Implement flexible work policies that allow employees to choose when and where they work, based on their individual needs and preferences. Promote inclusivity by fostering a culture of respect, diversity, and inclusion. Provide training on unconscious bias and create opportunities for underrepresented groups to advance within the organization. For example, Salesforce's commitment to diversity and inclusion has been recognized as a key factor in its resilient culture (Dallas, 2015).

6. Continuous Learning and Development

Continuous learning and development are essential for building resilience. Organizations that invest in the growth and development of their employees are better equipped to adapt to changing conditions and innovate in response to new challenges. Learning and development programs help employees acquire new skills, stay current with industry trends, and prepare for future opportunities (Manciagli, 2016).

Promoting a Learning Culture

Promote a culture of continuous learning by providing access to training programs, workshops, and online courses. Encourage employees to pursue professional development opportunities and support their efforts to gain new certifications and qualifications. Companies like IBM offer extensive learning and development programs to ensure their workforce remains adaptable and resilient (Riggio, 2018).

Strategies for Fostering Organizational Resilience

To cultivate a resilient organizational culture, leaders must implement strategies that address the key components of resilience. These strategies should be integrated into the organization's overall approach to management, leadership, and employee engagement.

1. Develop a Resilience Framework

A resilience framework provides a structured approach to building and sustaining resilience within the organization. This framework should outline the key components of resilience, set clear objectives, and establish metrics for measuring progress. It should also include action plans for addressing specific challenges and opportunities (Sull, 1999).

Components of a Resilience Framework

- **Vision and Purpose:** Clearly define the organization's vision and purpose, and communicate them to all stakeholders.
- **Leadership Commitment:** Ensure that leaders are committed to resilience and model resilient behaviors.

- **Communication:** Develop a comprehensive communication plan that includes regular updates and two-way feedback mechanisms.
- **Employee Empowerment:** Empower employees to take initiative and make decisions, and provide the necessary resources and support.
- **Flexible and Inclusive Environment:** Implement flexible work arrangements and promote inclusivity within the organization.
- **Continuous Learning:** Invest in learning and development programs to help employees acquire new skills and stay current with industry trends (Dallas, 2015).

2. Engage Employees in Resilience Building

Employee engagement is critical to building organizational resilience. Engaged employees are more likely to be committed to the organization's goals, take initiative, and contribute to problem-solving efforts. Leaders should involve employees in resilience-building activities and encourage their participation in decision-making processes (Manciagli, 2016).

Strategies for Employee Engagement

- **Involvement in Decision-Making:** Involve employees in strategic planning and decision-making processes. Solicit their input and feedback on key initiatives and challenges.
- **Resilience Training:** Provide training on resilience and stress management to help employees develop the skills needed to cope with adversity.
- **Recognition and Rewards:** Recognize and reward employees for their contributions to resilience-building efforts. Celebrate successes and acknowledge the efforts of individuals and teams (Riggio, 2018).

3. Foster a Culture of Collaboration

Collaboration is essential for building resilience, as it enables the organization to leverage diverse perspectives and expertise. A collaborative culture encourages teamwork, knowledge sharing, and collective problem-solving. Leaders should create opportunities for collaboration and foster an environment where employees feel comfortable working together (Sull, 1999).

Promoting Collaboration

- **Cross-Functional Teams:** Form cross-functional teams to address complex challenges and drive innovation. Include members from different departments and levels to ensure diverse perspectives and expertise.
- **Collaborative Tools:** Use collaborative tools and platforms, such as Slack, Microsoft Teams, and Asana, to facilitate communication and project management.
- **Team-Building Activities:** Organize team-building activities and events to strengthen relationships and foster a sense of camaraderie among employees (Dallas, 2015).

4. Enhance Organizational Agility

Organizational agility is the ability to respond quickly and effectively to changing conditions. Enhancing agility requires a combination of flexible structures, adaptive processes, and a mindset that embraces change. Leaders should implement practices that promote agility and enable the organization to pivot as needed (Manciagli, 2016).

Strategies for Enhancing Agility

- **Flexible Structures:** Implement flexible organizational structures that allow for rapid reconfiguration of teams and resources. Use matrix structures or agile frameworks to enhance responsiveness.
- **Adaptive Processes:** Develop adaptive processes that can be adjusted based on feedback and changing conditions. Use iterative approaches, such as agile project management, to enable continuous improvement.

- **Change Management:** Implement effective change management practices to help employees navigate transitions and embrace new ways of working. Provide training and support to ensure successful adoption of changes (Riggio, 2018).

5. Invest in Resilience Training and Development

Resilience training and development programs help employees build the skills needed to cope with stress, adapt to change, and thrive in challenging situations. These programs should be tailored to the specific needs of the organization and its workforce, and should include both individual and team-based components (Sull, 1999).

Designing Resilience Training Programs

- **Needs Assessment:** Conduct a needs assessment to identify the specific resilience skills needed within the organization. Use surveys, interviews, and performance data to gather insights.
- **Customized Training:** Develop customized training programs that address the identified needs and align with the organization's goals. Include a mix of in-person training, online courses, and hands-on workshops.
- **Ongoing Support:** Provide ongoing support and resources to help employees apply what they have learned. Offer coaching, mentoring, and access to online resources to reinforce training (Dallas, 2015).

6. Create a Supportive Work Environment

A supportive work environment enhances resilience by providing employees with the resources and support they need to succeed. This includes access to mental health resources, work-life balance initiatives, and a positive organizational culture. Leaders should prioritize employee well-being and create an environment where employees feel valued and supported (Manciagli, 2016).

Elements of a Supportive Work Environment

- **Mental Health Resources:** Provide access to mental health resources, such as employee assistance programs (EAPs), counseling services, and stress management workshops.
- **Work-Life Balance:** Promote work-life balance by offering flexible work arrangements, paid time off, and wellness programs. Encourage employees to take breaks and prioritize self-care.
- **Positive Culture:** Foster a positive organizational culture that values respect, inclusion, and collaboration. Recognize and celebrate employee achievements, and create opportunities for social connection (Riggio, 2018).

7. Monitor and Evaluate Resilience Efforts

Continuous monitoring and evaluation of resilience efforts are essential for ensuring their effectiveness. Leaders should establish metrics for measuring resilience, track progress, and make adjustments as needed. Regular assessments help identify areas for improvement and ensure that the organization remains resilient in the face of new challenges (Sull, 1999).

Metrics for Measuring Resilience

- **Employee Engagement:** Measure employee engagement levels through surveys and feedback mechanisms. High engagement is a key indicator of resilience.
- **Adaptability:** Assess the organization's ability to adapt to changes and respond to disruptions. Use metrics such as time to recovery, number of innovations, and speed of decision-making.
- **Well-being:** Monitor employee well-being through surveys and health assessments. Track indicators such as stress levels, job satisfaction, and work-life balance (Dallas, 2015).

Conducting Resilience Assessments

- **Regular Reviews:** Conduct regular reviews of resilience efforts to assess progress and identify areas for improvement. Involve key stakeholders in the review process to ensure comprehensive assessments.

- **Feedback Loops:** Establish feedback loops that allow employees to provide input on resilience initiatives. Use this feedback to refine and improve resilience strategies.
- **Continuous Improvement:** Use the insights gained from monitoring and evaluation to make continuous improvements to resilience efforts. Implement best practices and learn from successes and challenges (Manciagli, 2016).

Case Studies: Successful Resilience Building

Examining real-world examples of organizations that have successfully cultivated a resilient culture provides valuable insights and inspiration.

Case Study 1: Johnson & Johnson

Johnson & Johnson's commitment to resilience is exemplified by its response to the Tylenol crisis in the 1980s. The company's swift and transparent actions, including a nationwide recall and the introduction of tamper-resistant packaging, restored public trust and reinforced its resilient culture. Johnson & Johnson's focus on ethical leadership, effective communication, and employee empowerment played a crucial role in navigating the crisis (Sull, 1999).

Case Study 2: Southwest Airlines

Southwest Airlines' resilient culture has enabled it to navigate industry challenges and maintain a competitive edge. The company's focus on employee well-being, customer service, and operational efficiency has created a strong foundation for resilience. Southwest's leadership commitment, collaborative culture, and continuous improvement initiatives have been key to its success (Dallas, 2015).

Case Study 3: Unilever

Unilever's sustainability and resilience efforts have positioned it as a leader in corporate responsibility. The company's Sustainable Living Plan, which integrates social and environmental goals into its business strategy, has enhanced its resilience to market and environmental changes. Unilever's emphasis on innovation, stakeholder engagement, and long-term vision has driven its resilient culture (Manciagli, 2016).

Conclusion

Cultivating a resilient organizational culture is essential for long-term success in today's dynamic and uncertain business environment. By understanding the key components of resilience and implementing strategies that address these components, leaders can create an environment that not only survives but thrives amidst adversity.

The case studies of Johnson & Johnson, Southwest Airlines, and Unilever demonstrate the power of resilience and the benefits of a resilient culture. These organizations have successfully navigated challenges and maintained their competitive edge by fostering a culture of adaptability, engagement, and continuous improvement.

By adopting the strategies outlined in this chapter, leaders can build a resilient organizational culture that supports sustained performance and growth. Embracing resilience and fostering a supportive, innovative, and agile environment will enable organizations to navigate future challenges and seize new opportunities.

References

Benedict, A. (2007). 2007 change management survey report. Alexandria, VA: Society for Human Resource Management.

Dallas, H. J. (2015, October 22). Here are 4 ways leaders can deal with change. *Fortune*. Retrieved from http://fortune.com/2015/10/22/change-leaders-managers/

Manciagli, D. (2016, April 13). 4 biggest challenges facing business leaders today. *Biz Journals*. Retrieved from https://www.bizjournals.com/bizjournals/how-to/growth-strategies/2016/04/4-biggest-challenges-facing-business-leaders-today.html

Riggio, R. E. (2018, December 9). What is servant leadership and why does it matter? *Psychology Today*. Retrieved from https://www.psychologytoday.com/us/blog/cutting-edge-leadership/201812/what-is-servant-leadership-and-why-does-it-matter

Sull, D. (1999, July-August). Why good companies go bad. *Harvard Business Review*, 42–55. Retrieved from https://hbr.org/1999/07/why-good-companies-go-bad

CHAPTER 9

Strategic Decision-Making in Uncertain Times

Personal Narrative: Strategic Decision-Making in Uncertain Times

As explained, I've navigated the challenges of starting divisions in multiple companies, especially during uncertain times. The cyclical nature of our industry means that strategic decision-making is crucial for survival and growth, particularly during downturns.

At InnovateX, shortly after launching our new division, we faced a significant market downturn. Projects were delayed or canceled, and uncertainty loomed large. Drawing from my previous experiences, I knew that clear, strategic decision-making was essential to steer us through these turbulent times.

One of the first steps I took was conducting a thorough risk assessment. We identified our most vulnerable projects and explored ways to mitigate potential losses. I gathered input from my team, ensuring that we considered diverse perspectives and expertise in our decision-making process.

To conserve resources, we prioritized projects that promised the highest return on investment and deferred those that were less critical. This selective approach allowed us to focus our efforts and finances where they were most needed. We also renegotiated contracts with suppliers and subcontractors to reduce costs without compromising quality.

During this period, I emphasized the importance of maintaining strong relationships with our clients. Transparent communication about project statuses and our strategic plans helped build trust and reassurance. This proved invaluable when the market began to recover, as clients appreciated our honesty and commitment.

Internally, I took a page from my military days where we are always taught to know the job of the man above and below us. We invested in cross-training our team members, ensuring that they could adapt to different roles as needed. This flexibility not only kept our workforce engaged but also prepared us for a swift ramp-up once the market conditions improved.

One particularly tough decision involved temporarily scaling back our workforce. It was a difficult but necessary move to ensure the division's long-term viability. However, we made it a point to support affected employees with severance packages and assistance in finding new opportunities.

As the market started to rebound, our strategic decisions during the downturn positioned us well. We were able to quickly resume paused projects and secure new ones, thanks to our preserved resources and strengthened client relationships. Our division not only survived the bust but emerged stronger and more agile.

This experience underscored the importance of strategic decision-making in uncertain times. By conducting thorough risk assessments, prioritizing high-impact projects, maintaining client relationships, and investing in team adaptability, we navigated the downturn effectively and set the stage for future success.

Introduction

In an increasingly volatile and unpredictable business environment, strategic decision-making has become more critical than ever. Organizations must navigate complex challenges, respond to rapid changes, and anticipate future uncertainties to remain competitive and achieve sustainable growth. This chapter explores the principles of strategic decision-making in uncertain times, examines the role of data and analytics, and provides strategies for making informed and agile decisions. By understanding and implementing these strategies, leaders can guide their organizations through uncertainty and capitalize on emerging opportunities.

The Nature of Strategic Decision-Making

Strategic decision-making involves making choices that determine the direction and success of an organization. These decisions often have long-term implications and require careful consideration of various factors, including market trends, competitive dynamics, and internal capabilities (Riggio, 2018).

Understanding Strategic Decision-Making

Strategic decisions are typically high-stakes and involve significant resource allocation. They are made at the highest levels of the organization and require a comprehensive understanding of the external environment and internal strengths and weaknesses. Examples of strategic decisions include entering new markets, launching new products, and restructuring the organization (Sull, 1999).

Challenges in Strategic Decision-Making

Strategic decision-making is inherently challenging due to the complexity and uncertainty of the business environment. Common challenges include incomplete or ambiguous information, time constraints, conflicting priorities, and cognitive biases. Leaders must navigate these challenges to make informed and effective decisions (Dallas, 2015).

The Importance of Agility

Agility is a critical component of strategic decision-making in uncertain times. Agile decision-making involves the ability to quickly assess situations, make decisions, and adjust strategies as needed. Organizations that are agile can respond more effectively to changing conditions and capitalize on new opportunities (Manciagli, 2016).

The Role of Data and Analytics in Strategic Decision-Making

Data and analytics play a crucial role in enhancing the quality and effectiveness of strategic decision-making. By leveraging data-driven insights, organizations can make more informed decisions, reduce uncertainty, and improve outcomes (Sull, 1999).

Leveraging Big Data

Big data refers to the vast amounts of structured and unstructured data generated by various sources, including customer interactions, social media, sensors, and transactions. Analyzing big data can provide valuable insights into market trends, customer behavior, and operational performance. For example, retailers use big data analytics to forecast demand, optimize inventory, and personalize customer experiences (Dallas, 2015).

Predictive Analytics

Predictive analytics involves using historical data and statistical algorithms to predict future outcomes. This approach helps organizations anticipate trends, identify risks, and make proactive decisions. For instance, financial institutions use predictive analytics to assess credit risk, detect fraud, and optimize investment strategies (Manciagli, 2016).

Real-Time Analytics

Real-time analytics allows organizations to analyze data as it is generated, enabling faster and more responsive decision-making. This capability is particularly valuable in dynamic environments where conditions can change rapidly. For example, logistics companies use real-time analytics to monitor supply chain performance, track shipments, and optimize routes (Riggio, 2018).

Data Visualization

Data visualization tools help decision-makers understand complex data by presenting it in an easily interpretable format, such as charts, graphs, and dashboards. Visualizing data can reveal patterns and trends that may not be apparent in raw data, facilitating better strategic decisions. Companies like Tableau and Power BI offer powerful data visualization solutions that support decision-making (Sull, 1999).

Principles of Strategic Decision-Making

Effective strategic decision-making requires adherence to key principles that guide the decision-making process. These principles ensure that decisions are well-informed, aligned with organizational goals, and adaptable to changing conditions.

1. Define Clear Objectives

Clear objectives provide a foundation for strategic decision-making by establishing what the organization aims to achieve. Objectives should be specific, measurable, achievable, relevant, and time-bound (SMART). Clear objectives help align efforts, prioritize actions, and evaluate the success of decisions (Dallas, 2015).

Setting Strategic Objectives

Strategic objectives should be aligned with the organization's vision and mission. They should address key areas such as market growth, customer satisfaction, operational efficiency, and financial performance. For example, a technology company might set an objective to increase market share in a specific region by 20% within two years (Manciagli, 2016).

2. Gather and Analyze Relevant Information

Effective decision-making requires comprehensive and accurate information. Organizations should gather data from various sources, including market research, customer feedback, competitive analysis, and financial reports. Analyzing this information helps identify trends, opportunities, and risks (Riggio, 2018).

Information Gathering Techniques

- **Market Research:** Conduct surveys, focus groups, and interviews to gather insights into customer needs, preferences, and behaviors.
- **Competitive Analysis:** Analyze competitors' strengths, weaknesses, strategies, and market positions to identify opportunities and threats.
- **Financial Reports:** Review financial statements, budgets, and forecasts to assess the organization's financial health and identify trends (Sull, 1999).

3. Involve Key Stakeholders

Involving key stakeholders in the decision-making process ensures that diverse perspectives and expertise are considered. Stakeholders may include executives, managers, employees, customers, suppliers, and investors. Engaging stakeholders helps build consensus, gain buy-in, and enhance the quality of decisions (Dallas, 2015).

Stakeholder Engagement Strategies

- **Cross-Functional Teams:** Form cross-functional teams to bring together representatives from different departments and areas of expertise.
- **Workshops and Meetings:** Organize workshops and meetings to discuss strategic issues, gather input, and explore options.
- **Surveys and Feedback:** Use surveys and feedback mechanisms to solicit input from stakeholders and assess their perspectives (Manciagli, 2016).

4. Evaluate Options and Alternatives

Evaluating multiple options and alternatives allows organizations to explore different approaches and select the most effective course of action. This process involves assessing the potential impact, feasibility, and risks associated with each option (Riggio, 2018).

Techniques for Evaluating Options

- **SWOT Analysis:** Assess the strengths, weaknesses, opportunities, and threats related to each option.
- **Cost-Benefit Analysis:** Compare the costs and benefits of each option to determine their overall value.
- **Scenario Planning:** Develop and analyze different scenarios to understand the potential outcomes and implications of each option (Sull, 1999).

5. Make Informed Decisions

Informed decision-making involves selecting the option that best aligns with the organization's objectives, values, and resources. Decision-makers should consider both quantitative data and qualitative insights, balancing analytical rigor with intuition and judgment (Dallas, 2015).

Decision-Making Frameworks

- **Decision Matrix:** Use a decision matrix to evaluate options based on specific criteria and assign weights to each criterion.
- **Balanced Scorecard:** Apply the balanced scorecard framework to assess the impact of decisions across multiple dimensions, such as financial, customer, internal processes, and learning and growth.
- **Pros and Cons List:** Create a list of pros and cons for each option to facilitate a structured comparison and support decision-making (Manciagli, 2016).

6. Implement and Monitor Decisions

Successful implementation and monitoring are crucial for translating decisions into action and achieving desired outcomes. Organizations should develop detailed implementation plans, allocate resources, and establish metrics to track progress and measure success (Riggio, 2018).

Implementation Strategies

- **Action Plans:** Develop action plans that outline the steps, timelines, and responsibilities for implementing decisions.
- **Resource Allocation:** Ensure that adequate resources, including budget, personnel, and technology, are allocated to support implementation.
- **Change Management:** Implement change management practices to facilitate smooth transitions and address resistance (Sull, 1999).

Monitoring and Evaluation

- **Key Performance Indicators (KPIs):** Establish KPIs to measure the progress and success of decisions. Regularly review and update KPIs to ensure they remain relevant.
- **Progress Reviews:** Conduct regular progress reviews to assess the status of implementation and identify any issues or obstacles.
- **Continuous Improvement:** Use feedback and performance data to make continuous improvements to decisions and implementation efforts (Dallas, 2015).

Strategies for Making Strategic Decisions in Uncertain Times

Uncertainty adds complexity to strategic decision-making, requiring organizations to adopt strategies that enhance flexibility, resilience, and responsiveness. The following strategies can help leaders navigate uncertainty and make effective strategic decisions.

1. Scenario Planning

Scenario planning involves developing and analyzing different scenarios to anticipate potential future conditions and their impact on the organization. This approach helps organizations prepare for uncertainty and make more informed decisions (Manciagli, 2016).

Steps in Scenario Planning

- **Identify Key Drivers:** Identify the key drivers of change that could impact the organization, such as economic trends, technological advancements, and regulatory changes.
- **Develop Scenarios:** Create a range of plausible scenarios based on different combinations of key drivers. Each scenario should represent a distinct future state.
- **Analyze Scenarios:** Assess the potential impact of each scenario on the organization's objectives, strategies, and operations. Identify opportunities and risks associated with each scenario.
- **Develop Contingency Plans:** Develop contingency plans for each scenario, outlining the actions the organization will take if that scenario materializes. These plans should include specific initiatives, resource allocations, and timelines (Riggio, 2018).

Benefits of Scenario Planning

Scenario planning enhances strategic decision-making by providing a structured approach to anticipating and preparing for uncertainty. It helps organizations identify potential risks and opportunities, develop flexible strategies, and build resilience to changing conditions (Sull, 1999).

2. Agile Decision-Making

Agile decision-making involves making quick, iterative decisions and continuously adapting strategies based on feedback and changing conditions. This approach is well-suited to dynamic environments where uncertainty is high (Dallas, 2015).

Principles of Agile Decision-Making

- **Iterative Process:** Use an iterative decision-making process that involves making small, incremental decisions and continuously refining strategies.
- **Feedback Loops:** Establish feedback loops to gather input from stakeholders and assess the impact of decisions. Use this feedback to make adjustments and improvements.
- **Flexibility:** Maintain flexibility in decision-making, allowing for quick pivots and adjustments based on new information and changing conditions.
- **Collaboration:** Foster collaboration and cross-functional teamwork to leverage diverse perspectives and expertise in decision-making (Manciagli, 2016).

Implementing Agile Decision-Making

- **Short Decision Cycles:** Implement short decision cycles that allow for rapid decision-making and frequent reassessment of strategies.
- **Empowered Teams:** Empower teams to make decisions and take action quickly, without needing extensive approvals or bureaucratic processes.
- **Continuous Learning:** Foster a culture of continuous learning and improvement, encouraging employees to experiment, learn from failures, and share insights (Riggio, 2018).

3. Data-Driven Decision-Making

Data-driven decision-making involves using data and analytics to inform and guide strategic decisions. This approach helps reduce uncertainty and improve the accuracy and effectiveness of decisions (Sull, 1999).

Key Components of Data-Driven Decision-Making

- **Data Collection:** Collect data from a variety of sources, including internal systems, market research, customer feedback, and external databases.

- **Data Analysis:** Use advanced analytics techniques, such as predictive modeling, machine learning, and data visualization, to analyze data and generate insights.
- **Decision Support Systems:** Implement decision support systems (DSS) that provide real-time data, analytics, and recommendations to decision-makers.
- **Data Governance:** Establish data governance practices to ensure the accuracy, consistency, and security of data. This includes data quality controls, data privacy measures, and compliance with regulations (Dallas, 2015).

Best Practices for Data-Driven Decision-Making

- **Define Data Needs:** Clearly define the data needs and objectives for each decision. Identify the key metrics and data sources required to support decision-making.
- **Invest in Analytics Tools:** Invest in advanced analytics tools and technologies that enable comprehensive data analysis and visualization.
- **Train Decision-Makers:** Provide training and resources to decision-makers to help them effectively use data and analytics in their decision-making processes.
- **Foster a Data-Driven Culture:** Foster a culture that values data and evidence-based decision-making. Encourage employees to use data in their daily work and reward data-driven initiatives (Manciagli, 2016).

4. Risk Management

Effective risk management is essential for navigating uncertainty and making strategic decisions. Organizations should identify, assess, and mitigate risks to minimize their impact and ensure continuity (Riggio, 2018).

Risk Management Process

- **Risk Identification:** Identify potential risks that could impact the organization's objectives, strategies, and operations. Use techniques such as risk assessments, audits, and scenario analysis.
- **Risk Assessment:** Assess the likelihood and impact of each identified risk. Use qualitative and quantitative methods to evaluate risks and prioritize them based on their severity.
- **Risk Mitigation:** Develop and implement risk mitigation strategies to reduce the likelihood and impact of identified risks. This may include preventive measures, contingency plans, and risk transfer mechanisms (e.g., insurance).
- **Risk Monitoring:** Continuously monitor risks and their impact on the organization. Use key risk indicators (KRIs) to track changes and identify emerging risks. Regularly review and update risk management plans to ensure their effectiveness (Sull, 1999).

Integrating Risk Management with Strategic Decision-Making

Integrate risk management into the strategic decision-making process by incorporating risk assessments into decision evaluations. Use risk analysis to inform decision-making and ensure that strategies are resilient to potential disruptions (Dallas, 2015).

5. Fostering a Learning Organization

A learning organization continuously evolves by encouraging learning, knowledge sharing, and innovation. This approach enhances strategic decision-making by ensuring that the organization remains adaptable and responsive to change (Manciagli, 2016).

Characteristics of a Learning Organization

- **Continuous Learning:** Promote a culture of continuous learning and development. Encourage employees to pursue professional development opportunities and stay current with industry trends.

- **Knowledge Sharing:** Facilitate knowledge sharing and collaboration across the organization. Use tools and platforms to enable the exchange of ideas, insights, and best practices.
- **Innovation:** Foster a culture of innovation by encouraging experimentation, risk-taking, and creative problem-solving. Recognize and reward innovative ideas and initiatives.
- **Reflective Practice:** Encourage reflective practice by promoting regular reviews and assessments of strategies, processes, and outcomes. Use lessons learned to inform future decision-making (Riggio, 2018).

Strategies for Building a Learning Organization

- **Learning and Development Programs:** Implement comprehensive learning and development programs that address the needs of employees at all levels. Offer a mix of in-person training, online courses, and hands-on workshops.
- **Communities of Practice:** Create communities of practice (CoPs) where employees with shared interests and expertise can collaborate and learn from each other.
- **Knowledge Management Systems:** Invest in knowledge management systems that capture, store, and disseminate organizational knowledge. Use these systems to support decision-making and continuous improvement.
- **Leadership Development:** Develop leadership programs that equip leaders with the skills needed to foster a learning culture. Provide coaching, mentoring, and resources to support leadership development (Sull, 1999).

6. Strategic Foresight

Strategic foresight involves systematically exploring and anticipating future trends, challenges, and opportunities. This approach helps organizations prepare for uncertainty and make proactive strategic decisions (Dallas, 2015).

Techniques for Strategic Foresight

- **Trend Analysis:** Analyze current and emerging trends to identify potential future developments. Use tools such as PESTEL analysis (Political, Economic, Social, Technological, Environmental, and Legal) to assess the impact of these trends.
- **Environmental Scanning:** Conduct environmental scanning to monitor changes in the external environment. Use sources such as industry reports, news articles, and expert opinions to gather insights.
- **Delphi Method:** Use the Delphi method to gather input from a panel of experts on future trends and scenarios. This technique involves multiple rounds of questioning and feedback to reach a consensus.
- **Visioning:** Engage stakeholders in visioning exercises to imagine and articulate desired future states. Use these visions to guide strategic planning and decision-making (Manciagli, 2016).

Benefits of Strategic Foresight

Strategic foresight enhances decision-making by providing a long-term perspective and helping organizations anticipate and prepare for future challenges and opportunities. It supports proactive strategy development and reduces the impact of uncertainty (Riggio, 2018).

Case Studies: Effective Strategic Decision-Making

Examining real-world examples of organizations that have successfully navigated uncertainty and made effective strategic decisions provides valuable insights and inspiration.

Case Study 1: Procter & Gamble

Procter & Gamble's (P&G) decision to focus on its core brands during the 2008 financial crisis is a prime example of effective strategic decision-making. By divesting non-core businesses and investing in its strongest brands, P&G was able to streamline operations, reduce costs, and enhance profitability. This strategic shift enabled P&G to emerge stronger from the crisis and maintain its market leadership (Sull, 1999).

Case Study 2: General Electric

General Electric's (GE) decision to transform its business model by investing in digital technologies and renewable energy exemplifies strategic foresight and adaptability. Under the leadership of CEO Jeff Immelt, GE embraced the Industrial Internet of Things (IIoT) and launched GE Digital to drive innovation and growth. This strategic pivot positioned GE as a leader in the digital industrial sector and supported its long-term sustainability (Dallas, 2015).

Case Study 3: IBM

IBM's decision to shift its focus from hardware to cloud computing and AI is a testament to the power of strategic foresight and agility. Faced with declining hardware sales, IBM made bold investments in cloud services, data analytics, and cognitive computing. This strategic transformation enabled IBM to reinvent itself and remain competitive in the rapidly evolving technology landscape (Manciagli, 2016).

Conclusion

Strategic decision-making in uncertain times requires a combination of foresight, agility, data-driven insights, and effective risk management. By understanding and implementing the principles and strategies outlined in this chapter, leaders can navigate complexity and uncertainty, make informed decisions, and position their organizations for long-term success.

The case studies of Procter & Gamble, General Electric, and IBM demonstrate the power of effective strategic decision-making and the benefits of foresight, adaptability, and innovation. These organizations have successfully navigated uncertainty and maintained their competitive edge by making bold, informed, and agile strategic decisions.

By adopting the strategies outlined in this chapter, leaders can enhance their decision-making capabilities and guide their organizations through uncertain times. Embracing strategic foresight, leveraging data and analytics, fostering a learning culture, and implementing effective risk management practices will enable organizations to thrive in a dynamic and unpredictable business environment.

References

Benedict, A. (2007). 2007 change management survey report. Alexandria, VA: Society for Human Resource Management.

Dallas, H. J. (2015, October 22). Here are 4 ways leaders can deal with change. *Fortune*. Retrieved from http://fortune.com/2015/10/22/change-leaders-managers/

Manciagli, D. (2016, April 13). 4 biggest challenges facing business leaders today. *Biz Journals*. Retrieved from https://www.bizjournals.com/bizjournals/how-to/growth-strategies/2016/04/4-biggest-challenges-facing-business-leaders-today.html

Riggio, R. E. (2018, December 9). What is servant leadership and why does it matter? *Psychology Today*. Retrieved from https://www.psychologytoday.com/us/blog/cutting-edge-leadership/201812/what-is-servant-leadership-and-why-does-it-matter

Sull, D. (1999, July-August). Why good companies go bad. *Harvard Business Review*, 42–55. Retrieved from https://hbr.org/1999/07/why-good-companies-go-bad

CHAPTER 10

Leading Through Organizational Transformation

Personal Narrative: Leading Through Organizational Transformation

As the division head of multifamily construction, I've led divisions through significant changes, but one of the most impactful was the rebranding effort at InnovateX. Our fragmented identity was affecting our market position and employee morale, making a comprehensive rebranding necessary.

I involved my team from the start, gathering their input through workshops, which built buy-in and excitement. We collaborated with marketing to create a new brand that reflected our core values and future goals. Aligning this with ongoing projects was challenging, but regular updates and open communication helped ensure a smooth transition.

We updated project sites, launched a redesigned website, and rolled out new marketing materials, ensuring consistency across all touchpoints. Training sessions helped employees embody the new brand values, emphasizing that this was a commitment to excellence, not just a cosmetic change.

The rebranding culminated in a company-wide event to unveil our new identity and celebrate our future vision. Despite initial resistance, the transformation strengthened our market presence, improved client satisfaction, and boosted employee pride.

This experience highlighted the power of strong leadership and clear strategy in navigating organizational transformation. By involving the team and committing to a unified vision, we successfully rebranded and positioned ourselves for future success.

Introduction

Organizational transformation is a fundamental shift in the way an organization operates, often involving changes in structure, strategy, culture, and processes. Effective leadership is crucial for guiding an organization through these complex and often challenging changes. This chapter explores the principles of leading organizational transformation, examines the role of transformational leadership, and provides strategies for successfully implementing and sustaining transformation. By understanding and implementing these strategies, leaders can ensure that their organizations not only survive but thrive during periods of significant change.

The Nature of Organizational Transformation

Organizational transformation involves comprehensive changes that fundamentally alter the way an organization functions. These changes can be driven by various factors, including technological advancements, market dynamics, competitive pressures, regulatory shifts, and internal growth. Transformation is not just about making incremental improvements; it requires a fundamental rethinking of the organization's mission, vision, and strategies (Riggio, 2018).

Understanding Organizational Transformation

Organizational transformation is a holistic process that affects all aspects of the organization, including its structure, culture, processes, and people. It often involves multiple phases, including envisioning the future state, planning the transformation, executing the change, and sustaining the new way of working. Successful transformation requires a clear vision, strong leadership, effective communication, and robust change management practices (Sull, 1999).

Challenges in Organizational Transformation

Transformational change is inherently challenging due to its scope and complexity. Common challenges include resistance to change, cultural inertia, resource constraints, and maintaining morale and productivity during the transition. Leaders must navigate these challenges to ensure the successful implementation of transformation initiatives (Dallas, 2015).

The Importance of Transformational Leadership

Transformational leadership is essential for guiding organizations through significant changes. Transformational leaders inspire and motivate their teams, communicate a compelling vision, and foster a culture of innovation and adaptability. They play a crucial role in overcoming resistance, building commitment, and ensuring the successful execution of transformation initiatives (Manciagli, 2016).

Principles of Leading Organizational Transformation

Effective leadership during organizational transformation is guided by key principles that ensure the process is strategic, inclusive, and sustainable. These principles provide a framework for navigating the complexities of transformational change.

1. Articulate a Compelling Vision

A clear and compelling vision provides direction and motivation for the transformation effort. It helps align the organization's efforts and resources towards a common goal. Leaders must communicate the vision effectively, ensuring that it resonates with all stakeholders and inspires commitment (Riggio, 2018).

Developing the Vision

The vision for transformation should reflect the organization's core values and long-term aspirations. It should be ambitious yet achievable, providing a clear picture of the desired future state. For example, a manufacturing company undergoing digital transformation might envision becoming a leader in smart manufacturing through the adoption of advanced technologies like IoT and AI (Sull, 1999).

Communicating the Vision

Effective communication of the vision is critical for building buy-in and support. Leaders should use various communication channels, including town hall meetings, newsletters, and digital platforms, to share the vision with all stakeholders. They should also engage in active listening, addressing concerns and feedback to ensure alignment and commitment (Dallas, 2015).

2. Build a Strong Leadership Team

A strong and cohesive leadership team is essential for driving organizational transformation. This team should include leaders from different functions and levels, bringing diverse perspectives and expertise to the transformation effort. Collaboration and alignment within the leadership team are crucial for effective decision-making and execution (Manciagli, 2016).

Forming the Leadership Team

Form the leadership team by selecting individuals who possess the necessary skills, experience, and commitment to drive transformation. Ensure that the team includes representation from key functions, such as operations, finance, human resources, and technology. This diversity of expertise helps address the various aspects of the transformation (Riggio, 2018).

Fostering Collaboration and Alignment

Promote collaboration and alignment within the leadership team by establishing clear roles and responsibilities, setting common goals, and fostering open communication. Regular leadership meetings and workshops can help build trust and facilitate effective decision-making. For example, cross-functional leadership retreats can be used to align on strategic priorities and develop a unified approach to transformation (Sull, 1999).

3. Engage and Empower Employees

Employee engagement and empowerment are critical to the success of organizational transformation. Engaged employees are more likely to embrace change, contribute ideas, and support the transformation effort. Leaders should involve employees in the transformation process, providing opportunities for input and participation (Dallas, 2015).

Strategies for Employee Engagement

- **Involve Employees in Planning:** Involve employees in the planning phase by soliciting their input and feedback on the transformation strategy. Use surveys, focus groups, and workshops to gather insights and ideas.
- **Communicate Transparently:** Communicate transparently with employees about the goals, benefits, and challenges of the transformation. Provide regular updates and create opportunities for dialogue.
- **Recognize and Reward Contributions:** Recognize and reward employees who actively contribute to the transformation effort. Celebrate successes and acknowledge the efforts of individuals and teams (Manciagli, 2016).

Empowering Employees

Empower employees by providing them with the resources, training, and support they need to succeed in the transformed organization. Encourage autonomy and decision-making at all levels, and create a culture of trust and accountability. For example, organizations undergoing digital transformation might provide employees with training in new technologies and tools, enabling them to take ownership of digital initiatives (Riggio, 2018).

4. Foster a Culture of Innovation and Adaptability

A culture of innovation and adaptability is essential for sustaining organizational transformation. Leaders should encourage experimentation, risk-taking, and continuous improvement, creating an environment where new ideas can flourish and changes can be implemented effectively (Sull, 1999).

Promoting Innovation

Promote innovation by creating dedicated spaces and resources for experimentation, such as innovation labs or incubators. Encourage cross-functional collaboration and knowledge sharing, and provide incentives for innovative ideas. Recognize and celebrate successful innovations, and use failures as learning opportunities (Dallas, 2015).

Encouraging Adaptability

Encourage adaptability by fostering a growth mindset and resilience within the organization. Provide training and development programs that equip employees with the skills needed to navigate change. Use scenario planning and other techniques to prepare for different future conditions, enabling the organization to pivot as needed (Manciagli, 2016).

5. Implement Effective Change Management Practices

Effective change management practices are crucial for guiding the organization through the transformation process. These practices help minimize disruption, address resistance, and ensure that changes are implemented smoothly and sustainably (Riggio, 2018).

Change Management Framework

Develop a change management framework that outlines the key steps and activities for managing the transformation. This framework should include stakeholder analysis, communication plans, training programs, and metrics for measuring progress. For example, the ADKAR model (Awareness, Desire, Knowledge, Ability, Reinforcement) provides a structured approach to managing individual and organizational change (Sull, 1999).

The Prosci ADKAR® Model

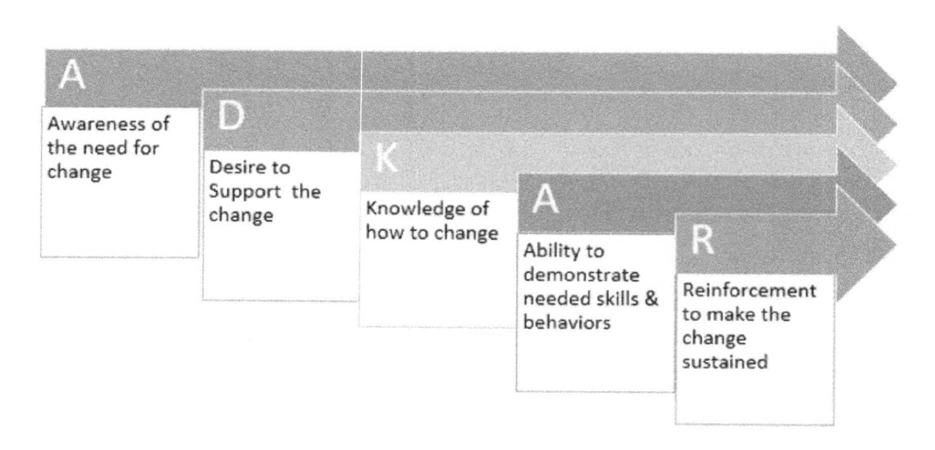

Change management model by Prosci
Image: AGS, Airiodion.com

Source: Hiatt, J. (2006). *ADKAR: A model for change in business, government, and our community*. Prosci Research.

Addressing Resistance

Address resistance to change by identifying the sources of resistance and developing strategies to mitigate them. Use techniques such as active listening, empathy, and negotiation to understand and address concerns. Provide support and resources to help employees navigate the transition, and involve them in finding solutions to challenges (Dallas, 2015).

6. Monitor and Evaluate Progress

Continuous monitoring and evaluation of the transformation process are essential for ensuring its success. Leaders should establish metrics for tracking progress, conduct regular reviews, and make adjustments as needed. This iterative approach helps identify issues early and allows for course corrections (Manciagli, 2016).

Establishing Metrics

Establish metrics that align with the transformation goals and objectives. These metrics should cover key areas such as financial performance, operational efficiency, customer satisfaction, and employee engagement. Use a balanced scorecard or similar tool to track progress across multiple dimensions (Riggio, 2018).

Conducting Reviews

Conduct regular reviews to assess the status of the transformation and identify any issues or obstacles. Use a combination of quantitative data and qualitative insights to evaluate progress. Involve key stakeholders in the review process to ensure a comprehensive assessment. For example, quarterly transformation review meetings can be used to discuss progress, share insights, and make necessary adjustments (Sull, 1999).

7. Sustain the Transformation

Sustaining the transformation requires ongoing effort and commitment. Leaders must ensure that the changes are embedded in the organization's culture, processes, and systems. This involves reinforcing new behaviors, continuously improving practices, and maintaining a focus on long-term goals (Dallas, 2015).

Reinforcing New Behaviors

Reinforce new behaviors by recognizing and rewarding those who demonstrate them. Use performance management systems to align individual goals with the transformation objectives. Provide ongoing training and development to support the adoption of new practices and technologies (Manciagli, 2016).

Continuous Improvement

Promote a culture of continuous improvement by encouraging employees to identify and implement enhancements to processes and practices. Use tools such as Lean and Six Sigma to drive continuous improvement initiatives. Regularly review and update transformation strategies to ensure they remain relevant and effective (Riggio, 2018).

The Role of Transformational Leadership

Transformational leadership is a style of leadership that inspires and motivates followers to achieve extraordinary outcomes. Transformational leaders are characterized by their vision, charisma, and ability to foster a culture of innovation and change. They play a crucial role in guiding organizations through transformation by creating a compelling vision, building trust, and empowering employees (Sull, 1999).

Characteristics of Transformational Leaders

Transformational leaders possess several key characteristics that enable them to lead successful transformation efforts. These include vision, inspiration, intellectual stimulation, and individualized consideration (Dallas, 2015).

Vision and Inspiration

Transformational leaders have a clear and compelling vision for the future. They communicate this vision with passion and enthusiasm, inspiring others to join them on the journey. Their ability to articulate a compelling vision helps align the organization's efforts and resources towards common goals (Manciagli, 2016).

Intellectual Stimulation

Transformational leaders encourage creativity, innovation, and critical thinking. They challenge the status quo and promote a culture of continuous learning and improvement. By fostering an environment where new ideas are valued, they enable the organization to adapt and innovate in response to changing conditions (Riggio, 2018).

Individualized Consideration

Transformational leaders show genuine concern for the needs and development of their followers. They provide personalized support and mentorship, helping employees grow and succeed. This individualized consideration builds trust and loyalty, enhancing employee engagement and commitment to the transformation effort (Sull, 1999).

Strategies for Developing Transformational Leadership

Organizations can develop transformational leadership by implementing targeted development programs and creating a supportive environment for transformational behaviors. These strategies include leadership training, mentorship, and fostering a culture of empowerment and innovation (Dallas, 2015).

Leadership Training Programs

Implement leadership training programs that focus on developing the skills and behaviors associated with transformational leadership. These programs should cover areas such as visioning, communication, emotional intelligence, and change management. Use a mix of classroom training, experiential learning, and coaching to develop well-rounded transformational leaders (Manciagli, 2016).

Mentorship and Coaching

Provide mentorship and coaching to emerging leaders to support their development. Pair experienced transformational leaders with high-potential employees to facilitate knowledge transfer and skill development. Use coaching to provide personalized feedback and guidance, helping leaders refine their transformational behaviors (Riggio, 2018).

Creating a Supportive Environment

Create an environment that supports and encourages transformational leadership behaviors. This includes fostering a culture of trust, collaboration, and innovation. Recognize and reward leaders who demonstrate transformational behaviors, and provide opportunities for them to share their experiences and insights with others (Sull, 1999).

Strategies for Successful Organizational Transformation

Successful organizational transformation requires a strategic and structured approach. The following strategies provide a roadmap for leaders to guide their organizations through transformation and achieve sustainable success.

1. Conduct a Thorough Assessment

A thorough assessment of the current state of the organization is the first step in the transformation process. This assessment helps identify the strengths, weaknesses, opportunities, and threats (SWOT) that will inform the transformation strategy (Dallas, 2015).

SWOT Analysis

Conduct a SWOT analysis to evaluate the organization's internal strengths and weaknesses, as well as external opportunities and threats. Use this analysis to identify areas for improvement and prioritize transformation initiatives. For example, a healthcare organization might identify a need to enhance patient care through digital health technologies (Manciagli, 2016).

Stakeholder Analysis

Conduct a stakeholder analysis to identify key stakeholders and assess their influence, interests, and potential impact on the transformation. Develop strategies to engage and communicate with stakeholders throughout the transformation process. For example, involving frontline employees in planning and decision-making can enhance buy-in and support (Riggio, 2018).

2. Develop a Comprehensive Transformation Plan

A comprehensive transformation plan provides a roadmap for achieving the desired future state. This plan should outline the key initiatives, timelines, resources, and metrics for the transformation effort (Sull, 1999).

Key Components of a Transformation Plan

- **Vision and Objectives:** Clearly define the vision and objectives of the transformation, aligning them with the organization's long-term goals.
- **Initiatives and Projects:** Identify the key initiatives and projects that will drive the transformation. Prioritize these initiatives based on their potential impact and feasibility.
- **Resources and Budget:** Allocate the necessary resources, including budget, personnel, and technology, to support the transformation initiatives.
- **Timelines and Milestones:** Establish timelines and milestones for each initiative, ensuring that progress is tracked and adjustments are made as needed.
- **Metrics and KPIs:** Define metrics and key performance indicators (KPIs) to measure the success of the transformation. Use these metrics to monitor progress and make data-driven decisions (Dallas, 2015).

3. Communicate Effectively

Effective communication is critical for building support and ensuring alignment throughout the transformation process. Leaders should develop a communication plan that includes regular updates, two-way feedback mechanisms, and multiple channels for disseminating information (Manciagli, 2016).

Communication Strategies

- **Regular Updates:** Provide regular updates on the progress of the transformation, highlighting key milestones, successes, and challenges. Use newsletters, emails, and digital platforms to keep stakeholders informed.
- **Two-Way Feedback:** Establish two-way feedback mechanisms, such as surveys, town hall meetings, and focus groups, to gather

input and address concerns. Act on the feedback received to demonstrate responsiveness and build trust.

- **Tailored Messaging:** Tailor communication messages to different stakeholder groups, ensuring that the information is relevant and meaningful. Use stories and examples to illustrate the benefits and impact of the transformation (Riggio, 2018).

4. Foster a Culture of Accountability

A culture of accountability ensures that individuals and teams take ownership of their roles and responsibilities in the transformation effort. Leaders should set clear expectations, provide regular feedback, and hold people accountable for their performance (Sull, 1999).

Setting Clear Expectations

Set clear expectations for performance and behavior during the transformation. Communicate these expectations through performance management systems, goal-setting processes, and regular check-ins. For example, establish specific targets for project completion, quality, and customer satisfaction (Dallas, 2015).

Providing Feedback and Recognition

Provide regular feedback and recognition to reinforce desired behaviors and performance. Use formal and informal feedback mechanisms to address issues and celebrate successes. Recognize and reward individuals and teams who demonstrate exceptional commitment and contributions to the transformation (Manciagli, 2016).

5. Invest in Training and Development

Training and development are essential for equipping employees with the skills and knowledge needed to succeed in the transformed organization. Leaders should invest in comprehensive training programs that address both technical and soft skills (Riggio, 2018).

Training Program Design

Design training programs that align with the transformation goals and address the specific needs of employees. Use a mix of in-person training, online courses, and hands-on workshops to provide a well-rounded learning experience. For example, a company implementing new technology might offer training on the technical aspects of the technology as well as change management skills (Sull, 1999).

Ongoing Support and Development

Provide ongoing support and development opportunities to ensure that employees continue to grow and adapt to the transformed organization. Offer coaching, mentoring, and access to online resources to reinforce learning. Use development plans to track progress and identify areas for further improvement (Dallas, 2015).

6. Monitor Progress and Adapt

Continuous monitoring and adaptation are essential for ensuring the success and sustainability of the transformation. Leaders should establish mechanisms for tracking progress, evaluating outcomes, and making necessary adjustments (Manciagli, 2016).

Progress Monitoring

Establish a system for monitoring the progress of transformation initiatives. Use metrics and KPIs to track performance and identify areas for improvement. Conduct regular progress reviews to assess the status of initiatives and make data-driven decisions (Riggio, 2018).

Adaptive Leadership

Practice adaptive leadership by remaining flexible and responsive to changing conditions. Use feedback and performance data to inform decision-making and adjust strategies as needed. Encourage a culture of continuous improvement and innovation, where employees are empowered to identify and implement enhancements (Sull, 1999).

7. Celebrate Successes and Learn from Failures

Celebrating successes and learning from failures are critical components of sustaining the transformation effort. Leaders should recognize and reward achievements, while also fostering a culture of learning and improvement (Dallas, 2015).

Celebrating Successes

Celebrate successes by acknowledging and rewarding individuals and teams who contribute to the transformation effort. Use formal recognition programs, awards, and public celebrations to highlight achievements. Share success stories and best practices to inspire and motivate others (Manciagli, 2016).

Learning from Failures

Encourage a culture of learning by viewing failures as opportunities for growth and improvement. Conduct post-mortem analyses to understand the root causes of failures and identify lessons learned. Use these insights to inform future initiatives and enhance the organization's resilience (Riggio, 2018).

Case Studies: Successful Organizational Transformation

Examining real-world examples of organizations that have successfully navigated transformation provides valuable insights and inspiration.

Case Study 1: Microsoft

Microsoft's transformation under CEO Satya Nadella is a prime example of successful organizational transformation. By shifting the company's focus to cloud computing and fostering a culture of innovation and collaboration, Nadella led Microsoft to new heights. The company's emphasis on customer-centricity, continuous learning, and agility has been key to its success (Sull, 1999).

Case Study 2: Starbucks

Starbucks' transformation during the 2008 financial crisis illustrates the power of visionary leadership and a strong corporate culture. Under the leadership of Howard Schultz, Starbucks refocused on its core values, improved customer experience, and innovated its product offerings. The company's commitment to employee engagement and community impact has been central to its sustained success (Dallas, 2015).

Case Study 3: IBM

IBM's shift from hardware to cloud computing and AI showcases the importance of strategic foresight and adaptability. By investing in new technologies and transforming its business model, IBM successfully navigated industry changes and maintained its competitive edge. The company's focus on continuous innovation and customer-centricity has driven its transformation (Manciagli, 2016).

Conclusion

Leading organizational transformation requires a combination of visionary leadership, strategic planning, effective communication, and a commitment to continuous improvement. By understanding and implementing the principles and strategies outlined in this chapter, leaders can guide their organizations through transformation and achieve sustainable success.

The case studies of Microsoft, Starbucks, and IBM demonstrate the power of effective leadership and the benefits of a comprehensive, strategic approach to transformation. These organizations have successfully navigated significant changes and maintained their competitive edge by fostering a culture of innovation, engagement, and resilience.

By adopting the strategies outlined in this chapter, leaders can build a foundation for successful organizational transformation. Embracing transformational leadership, engaging and empowering employees, fostering a culture of innovation, and implementing effective change management practices will enable organizations to thrive in a dynamic and rapidly changing business environment.

References

Benedict, A. (2007). 2007 change management survey report. Alexandria, VA: Society for Human Resource Management.

Dallas, H. J. (2015, October 22). Here are 4 ways leaders can deal with change. *Fortune*. Retrieved from http://fortune.com/2015/10/22/change-leaders-managers/

Manciagli, D. (2016, April 13). 4 biggest challenges facing business leaders today. *Biz Journals*. Retrieved from https://www.bizjournals.com/bizjournals/how-to/growth-strategies/2016/04/4-biggest-challenges-facing-business-leaders-today.html

Riggio, R. E. (2018, December 9). What is servant leadership and why does it matter? *Psychology Today*. Retrieved from https://www.psychologytoday.com/us/blog/cutting-edge-leadership/201812/what-is-servant-leadership-and-why-does-it-matter

Sull, D. (1999, July-August). Why good companies go bad. *Harvard Business Review*, 42–55. Retrieved from https://hbr.org/1999/07/why-good-companies-go-bad

CHAPTER 11

Building and Sustaining Innovation

Personal Narrative: Building and Sustaining Innovation

As the division head of multifamily construction, I've started divisions in multiple companies with a focus on innovation. At InnovateX, we needed to break free from traditional methods that stifled creativity.

I initiated regular brainstorming sessions and launched a pilot project using modular construction techniques. Despite initial skepticism, the pilot's success demonstrated faster completion times and reduced waste, convincing the team of its benefits.

To sustain innovation, I established an "Innovation Fund" for new technologies like drones and virtual reality, which improved efficiency and kept the team engaged. Cross-functional workshops further fostered creativity, breaking down silos and generating fresh ideas.

Recognizing and rewarding innovative efforts through an annual "Innovation Awards" ceremony motivated employees and created a sense of pride. This culture of innovation allowed us to lead in the industry, continuously improving and staying competitive.

Building and sustaining innovation at InnovateX required a deliberate strategy and a supportive environment, ensuring long-term success and adaptability in the multifamily construction sector.

This focus on innovation positioned us for long-term success, enabling us to tackle challenges with new approaches and stay ahead in the competitive multifamily construction industry.

Introduction

Innovation is the lifeblood of organizational growth and long-term success. In a rapidly changing business environment, the ability to innovate continuously and effectively is crucial for maintaining a competitive edge. This chapter explores the principles of building and sustaining innovation within an organization, examines the role of leadership in fostering an innovative culture, and provides strategies for implementing and managing innovation processes. By understanding and applying these principles and strategies, leaders can create an environment that nurtures creativity, drives continuous improvement, and delivers sustained value.

The Importance of Innovation

Innovation involves the development and implementation of new ideas, processes, products, or services that create value for customers and the organization. It is essential for driving growth, enhancing competitiveness, and responding to changing market demands (Riggio, 2018).

Types of Innovation

Innovation can take many forms, each with its own impact and implications for the organization. The main types of innovation include:

- **Product Innovation:** Developing new products or improving existing ones to meet customer needs and preferences. For example, Apple's introduction of the iPhone revolutionized the mobile phone industry.
- **Process Innovation:** Enhancing or redesigning business processes to increase efficiency, reduce costs, or improve quality. For instance, Toyota's implementation of lean manufacturing principles transformed automotive production.
- **Business Model Innovation:** Creating new ways to deliver value to customers and generate revenue. Netflix's shift from DVD rentals to a streaming service is a prime example.

- **Service Innovation:** Introducing new or improved services to enhance customer experience and satisfaction. Amazon's introduction of Prime membership services, including free shipping and streaming, exemplifies service innovation (Sull, 1999).

Challenges of Innovation

While innovation is critical for success, it also presents several challenges. These include resistance to change, resource constraints, risk aversion, and maintaining alignment with organizational goals. Leaders must address these challenges to create an environment that supports and sustains innovation (Dallas, 2015).

The Role of Leadership in Innovation

Leadership plays a pivotal role in fostering a culture of innovation. Leaders must inspire creativity, encourage risk-taking, and provide the resources and support needed to drive innovative initiatives. Transformational leadership, in particular, is essential for nurturing innovation by creating a vision, empowering employees, and promoting a culture of continuous improvement (Manciagli, 2016).

Principles of Building and Sustaining Innovation

Effective innovation requires adherence to key principles that guide the development and implementation of innovative ideas. These principles ensure that innovation efforts are strategic, inclusive, and sustainable.

1. Foster a Culture of Innovation

A culture of innovation is one where creativity, experimentation, and continuous improvement are encouraged and valued. Leaders must create an environment that supports innovation and empowers employees to contribute new ideas (Riggio, 2018).

Creating an Innovative Culture

To foster a culture of innovation, leaders should promote the following practices:

- **Encourage Creativity:** Provide opportunities for employees to brainstorm and develop new ideas. Create dedicated spaces for innovation, such as innovation labs or idea rooms.
- **Promote Collaboration:** Facilitate cross-functional collaboration and knowledge sharing. Encourage employees from different departments to work together on innovation projects.
- **Celebrate Failure:** Recognize that failure is a natural part of the innovation process. Encourage employees to take risks and learn from their mistakes.
- **Reward Innovation:** Implement recognition and reward programs to incentivize innovative thinking. Celebrate successful innovations and acknowledge the contributions of employees (Sull, 1999).

2. Align Innovation with Strategic Goals

Innovation efforts should be aligned with the organization's strategic goals to ensure that they contribute to long-term success. Leaders must identify priority areas for innovation and allocate resources accordingly (Dallas, 2015).

Strategic Alignment

Aligning innovation with strategic goals involves the following steps:

- **Define Innovation Priorities:** Identify key areas where innovation can drive the most value, such as new product development, process improvements, or market expansion.
- **Set Clear Objectives:** Establish clear, measurable objectives for innovation initiatives that align with the organization's overall strategy.

- **Allocate Resources:** Ensure that sufficient resources, including budget, personnel, and technology, are allocated to support innovation efforts.
- **Monitor Progress:** Regularly review the progress of innovation initiatives to ensure alignment with strategic goals and make adjustments as needed (Manciagli, 2016).

3. Provide Resources and Support

Innovation requires investment in resources and support systems to enable the development and implementation of new ideas. Leaders must ensure that employees have access to the tools, training, and funding needed to drive innovation (Riggio, 2018).

Supporting Innovation

Support innovation by providing the following resources and support:

- **Funding:** Allocate budget for innovation projects and initiatives. Consider establishing an innovation fund to support high-potential ideas.
- **Training:** Provide training and development programs to equip employees with the skills needed for innovation. Offer workshops on creativity, design thinking, and problem-solving.
- **Technology:** Invest in technology and tools that facilitate innovation, such as collaborative software, prototyping tools, and data analytics platforms.
- **Mentorship:** Establish mentorship programs to support employees in their innovation efforts. Pair experienced innovators with emerging talent to provide guidance and support (Sull, 1999).

4. Implement Effective Innovation Processes

Effective innovation processes ensure that new ideas are systematically developed, evaluated, and implemented. Leaders must establish structured processes for managing innovation, from idea generation to commercialization (Dallas, 2015).

Innovation Process Framework

An effective innovation process framework includes the following stages:

- **Idea Generation:** Encourage the generation of new ideas from various sources, including employees, customers, and partners. Use techniques such as brainstorming, crowdsourcing, and ideation workshops.
- **Idea Evaluation:** Evaluate ideas based on criteria such as feasibility, market potential, and alignment with strategic goals. Use a structured evaluation process to prioritize high-potential ideas.
- **Development:** Develop selected ideas into prototypes or pilot projects. Use iterative development approaches, such as agile or lean startup methodologies, to refine and test ideas.
- **Implementation:** Implement successful prototypes or pilots at scale. Develop detailed implementation plans, allocate resources, and establish timelines for execution.
- **Commercialization:** Commercialize new products, services, or processes by launching them to the market. Develop marketing and sales strategies to promote adoption and drive growth (Manciagli, 2016).

5. Encourage Collaboration and Open Innovation

Collaboration and open innovation involve leveraging external partnerships and networks to enhance innovation efforts. By engaging with external stakeholders, organizations can access new ideas, technologies, and markets (Riggio, 2018).

Collaborative Innovation

Foster collaborative innovation through the following practices:

- **Partnerships:** Develop partnerships with other organizations, including startups, research institutions, and industry consortia. Collaborate on joint innovation projects and share knowledge and resources.

- **Crowdsourcing:** Use crowdsourcing platforms to gather ideas and solutions from a broader community. Engage customers, suppliers, and other stakeholders in the innovation process.

- **Innovation Ecosystems:** Participate in innovation ecosystems, such as industry clusters or innovation hubs. Engage with other organizations and experts to exchange ideas and collaborate on innovation initiatives (Sull, 1999).

6. Measure and Evaluate Innovation

Measuring and evaluating innovation efforts is crucial for understanding their impact and making data-driven decisions. Leaders must establish metrics and evaluation processes to track the performance of innovation initiatives (Dallas, 2015).

Innovation Metrics

Establish metrics to measure the success of innovation efforts, including:

- **Input Metrics:** Track resources invested in innovation, such as R&D spending, number of innovation projects, and employee time dedicated to innovation.

- **Process Metrics:** Measure the effectiveness of innovation processes, such as the number of ideas generated, evaluated, and implemented.

- **Output Metrics:** Assess the outcomes of innovation initiatives, such as new product launches, revenue growth, cost savings, and customer satisfaction.

- **Impact Metrics:** Evaluate the long-term impact of innovation on the organization's performance and competitiveness. Consider metrics such as market share, profitability, and brand strength (Manciagli, 2016).

Evaluation Processes

Implement evaluation processes to assess the performance of innovation initiatives:

- **Regular Reviews:** Conduct regular reviews of innovation projects to track progress and identify areas for improvement. Use a combination of quantitative data and qualitative insights to evaluate performance.
- **Feedback Loops:** Establish feedback loops to gather input from employees, customers, and other stakeholders. Use feedback to refine and improve innovation processes and outcomes.
- **Continuous Improvement:** Use the insights gained from measurement and evaluation to drive continuous improvement. Implement best practices and lessons learned to enhance future innovation efforts (Riggio, 2018).

The Role of Transformational Leadership in Innovation

Transformational leadership is essential for fostering and sustaining innovation within an organization. Transformational leaders inspire and motivate their teams, create a vision for the future, and foster a culture of creativity and continuous improvement (Sull, 1999).

Characteristics of Transformational Leaders

Transformational leaders possess several key characteristics that enable them to drive innovation:

- **Vision:** Transformational leaders have a clear and compelling vision for the future. They communicate this vision with passion and enthusiasm, inspiring others to join them on the journey.

- **Inspiration:** Transformational leaders inspire their teams by setting high expectations and challenging them to achieve their full potential. They provide encouragement and support, fostering a sense of purpose and commitment.
- **Intellectual Stimulation:** Transformational leaders encourage creativity, innovation, and critical thinking. They challenge the status quo and promote a culture of continuous learning and improvement.
- **Individualized Consideration:** Transformational leaders show genuine concern for the needs and development of their followers. They provide personalized support and mentorship, helping employees grow and succeed (Dallas, 2015).

Strategies for Developing Transformational Leadership

Organizations can develop transformational leadership by implementing targeted development programs and creating a supportive environment for transformational behaviors (Manciagli, 2016).

Leadership Development Programs

Implement leadership development programs that focus on developing the skills and behaviors associated with transformational leadership. These programs should cover areas such as visioning, communication, emotional intelligence, and change management. Use a mix of classroom training, experiential learning, and coaching to develop well-rounded transformational leaders (Riggio, 2018).

Mentorship and Coaching

Provide mentorship and coaching to emerging leaders to support their development. Pair experienced transformational leaders with high-potential employees to facilitate knowledge transfer and skill development. Use coaching to provide personalized feedback and guidance, helping leaders refine their transformational behaviors (Sull, 1999).

Creating a Supportive Environment

Create an environment that supports and encourages transformational leadership behaviors. This includes fostering a culture of trust, collaboration, and innovation. Recognize and reward leaders who demonstrate transformational behaviors, and provide opportunities for them to share their experiences and insights with others (Dallas, 2015).

Strategies for Implementing and Managing Innovation

Implementing and managing innovation requires a strategic and structured approach. The following strategies provide a roadmap for leaders to build and sustain innovation within their organizations.

1. Establish an Innovation Strategy

An innovation strategy provides a clear framework for guiding innovation efforts. It outlines the organization's vision, priorities, and objectives for innovation, ensuring that efforts are aligned with strategic goals (Manciagli, 2016).

Components of an Innovation Strategy

- **Vision and Objectives:** Define the vision and objectives for innovation, aligning them with the organization's overall strategy. This includes identifying key areas where innovation can drive the most value.

- **Innovation Portfolio:** Develop an innovation portfolio that includes a mix of incremental, breakthrough, and transformative innovations. Allocate resources and funding based on the potential impact and risk of each initiative.

- **Resource Allocation:** Ensure that sufficient resources, including budget, personnel, and technology, are allocated to support innovation efforts. Consider establishing an innovation fund to support high-potential ideas.

- **Governance:** Establish governance structures to oversee innovation efforts and ensure alignment with strategic goals. This includes creating innovation committees or councils to provide oversight and guidance (Riggio, 2018).

2. Create an Innovation Ecosystem

An innovation ecosystem involves building a network of internal and external stakeholders to support and enhance innovation efforts. This ecosystem includes employees, customers, partners, suppliers, and other collaborators (Sull, 1999).

Building an Innovation Ecosystem

- **Internal Collaboration:** Foster collaboration and knowledge sharing within the organization. Create cross-functional teams and innovation hubs to encourage the exchange of ideas and expertise.
- **External Partnerships:** Develop partnerships with external organizations, including startups, research institutions, and industry consortia. Collaborate on joint innovation projects and share knowledge and resources.
- **Customer Engagement:** Engage customers in the innovation process by gathering feedback, conducting focus groups, and involving them in co-creation initiatives. Use customer insights to inform and drive innovation efforts.
- **Supplier Collaboration:** Collaborate with suppliers to identify and implement innovative solutions. Leverage supplier expertise and resources to enhance innovation initiatives (Dallas, 2015).

3. Implement Agile and Lean Methodologies

Agile and lean methodologies provide structured approaches for managing innovation projects. These methodologies emphasize iterative development, continuous improvement, and customer feedback (Manciagli, 2016).

Agile Methodology

Agile methodology involves breaking down innovation projects into smaller, manageable tasks and using iterative cycles (sprints) to develop and refine ideas. Key principles of agile include:

- **Customer-Centric:** Focus on delivering value to customers through continuous feedback and iterative development.
- **Collaboration:** Foster collaboration and communication within cross-functional teams.
- **Flexibility:** Adapt to changing requirements and feedback, allowing for quick pivots and adjustments.
- **Transparency:** Use visual tools, such as Kanban boards, to track progress and ensure transparency (Riggio, 2018).

Lean Methodology

Lean methodology focuses on maximizing value and minimizing waste. Key principles of lean include:

- **Value Stream Mapping:** Identify and map the value stream to understand the flow of value and eliminate waste.
- **Continuous Improvement:** Foster a culture of continuous improvement by encouraging employees to identify and implement enhancements.
- **Just-In-Time:** Produce only what is needed, when it is needed, to reduce inventory and increase efficiency.
- **Empowerment:** Empower employees to take ownership of processes and make decisions that drive improvement (Sull, 1999).

4. Develop a Robust Idea Management System

An idea management system provides a structured approach for capturing, evaluating, and implementing new ideas. This system ensures that valuable ideas are identified, prioritized, and developed effectively (Dallas, 2015).

Components of an Idea Management System

- **Idea Submission:** Create platforms for employees, customers, and partners to submit ideas. Use digital tools, such as idea management software, to facilitate submission and tracking.
- **Idea Evaluation:** Establish criteria and processes for evaluating ideas based on factors such as feasibility, market potential, and alignment with strategic goals. Use a combination of quantitative and qualitative assessments.
- **Idea Development:** Develop selected ideas into prototypes or pilot projects. Use iterative development approaches to refine and test ideas.
- **Implementation:** Implement successful prototypes or pilots at scale. Develop detailed implementation plans, allocate resources, and establish timelines for execution.
- **Recognition and Rewards:** Recognize and reward individuals and teams who contribute valuable ideas. Implement recognition programs to incentivize innovative thinking (Manciagli, 2016).

5. Leverage Technology and Digital Tools

Technology and digital tools play a crucial role in enabling and enhancing innovation efforts. Leaders must invest in the right tools and technologies to support the development and implementation of new ideas (Riggio, 2018).

Technology and Tools for Innovation

- **Collaboration Platforms:** Use collaboration platforms, such as Slack, Microsoft Teams, and Asana, to facilitate communication and teamwork.
- **Prototyping Tools:** Invest in prototyping tools, such as 3D printers and software, to enable rapid development and testing of ideas.

- **Data Analytics:** Leverage data analytics to gain insights into customer behavior, market trends, and operational performance. Use these insights to inform innovation efforts.
- **Artificial Intelligence:** Explore the use of artificial intelligence (AI) to enhance innovation. AI can be used for tasks such as predictive analytics, natural language processing, and automation.
- **Cloud Computing:** Use cloud computing to provide scalable and flexible resources for innovation projects. Cloud platforms enable rapid development, testing, and deployment of new ideas (Sull, 1999).

6. Foster a Learning Organization

A learning organization continuously evolves by encouraging learning, knowledge sharing, and innovation. This approach enhances the organization's ability to adapt and innovate in response to changing conditions (Dallas, 2015).

Characteristics of a Learning Organization

- **Continuous Learning:** Promote a culture of continuous learning and development. Encourage employees to pursue professional development opportunities and stay current with industry trends.
- **Knowledge Sharing:** Facilitate knowledge sharing and collaboration across the organization. Use tools and platforms to enable the exchange of ideas, insights, and best practices.
- **Innovation:** Foster a culture of innovation by encouraging experimentation, risk-taking, and creative problem-solving. Recognize and reward innovative ideas and initiatives.
- **Reflective Practice:** Encourage reflective practice by promoting regular reviews and assessments of strategies, processes, and outcomes. Use lessons learned to inform future innovation efforts (Manciagli, 2016).

Strategies for Building a Learning Organization

- **Learning and Development Programs:** Implement comprehensive learning and development programs that address the needs of employees at all levels. Offer a mix of in-person training, online courses, and hands-on workshops.
- **Communities of Practice:** Create communities of practice (CoPs) where employees with shared interests and expertise can collaborate and learn from each other.
- **Knowledge Management Systems:** Invest in knowledge management systems that capture, store, and disseminate organizational knowledge. Use these systems to support decision-making and continuous improvement.
- **Leadership Development:** Develop leadership programs that equip leaders with the skills needed to foster a learning culture. Provide coaching, mentoring, and resources to support leadership development (Riggio, 2018).

Case Studies: Building and Sustaining Innovation

Examining real-world examples of organizations that have successfully built and sustained innovation provides valuable insights and inspiration.

Case Study 1: Google

Google's culture of innovation has been instrumental in its success. The company encourages employees to spend 20% of their time on passion projects, leading to the development of products like Gmail and Google News. Google's focus on collaboration, risk-taking, and continuous learning has created an environment where innovation thrives (Sull, 1999).

Case Study 2: Tesla

Tesla's commitment to innovation has revolutionized the automotive industry. The company's focus on electric vehicles, autonomous driving, and renewable energy solutions has set new standards for sustainability and performance. Tesla's culture of innovation, driven by visionary leadership and a relentless pursuit of excellence, has enabled it to continuously push the boundaries of what is possible (Dallas, 2015).

Case Study 3: 3M

3M's innovation strategy has led to the development of iconic products such as Post-it Notes and Scotch Tape. The company fosters a culture of innovation by encouraging employees to dedicate 15% of their time to exploring new ideas. 3M's focus on collaboration, customer insights, and continuous improvement has driven its sustained success in innovation (Manciagli, 2016).

Conclusion

Building and sustaining innovation is essential for long-term success in today's dynamic and competitive business environment. By understanding and applying the principles and strategies outlined in this chapter, leaders can create an environment that nurtures creativity, drives continuous improvement, and delivers sustained value.

The case studies of Google, Tesla, and 3M demonstrate the power of effective innovation and the benefits of a strategic, collaborative approach. These organizations have successfully built and sustained innovation by fostering a culture of creativity, aligning innovation with strategic goals, and leveraging technology and partnerships.

By adopting the strategies outlined in this chapter, leaders can enhance their organization's ability to innovate and achieve sustainable growth. Embracing a culture of innovation, providing the necessary resources and support, implementing effective processes, and fostering a learning organization will enable organizations to thrive in a rapidly changing business landscape.

References

Benedict, A. (2007). 2007 change management survey report. Alexandria, VA: Society for Human Resource Management.

Dallas, H. J. (2015, October 22). Here are 4 ways leaders can deal with change. *Fortune*. Retrieved from http://fortune.com/2015/10/22/change-leaders-managers/

Manciagli, D. (2016, April 13). 4 biggest challenges facing business leaders today. *Biz Journals*. Retrieved from https://www.bizjournals.com/bizjournals/how-to/growth-strategies/2016/04/4-biggest-challenges-facing-business-leaders-today.html

Riggio, R. E. (2018, December 9). What is servant leadership and why does it matter? *Psychology Today*. Retrieved from https://www.psychologytoday.com/us/blog/cutting-edge-leadership/201812/what-is-servant-leadership-and-why-does-it-matter

Sull, D. (1999, July-August). Why good companies go bad. *Harvard Business Review*, 42–55. Retrieved from https://hbr.org/1999/07/why-good-companies-go-bad

CHAPTER 12

Developing Future Leaders

Personal Narrative: Developing Future Leaders

As the division head of multifamily construction, I've had the privilege of starting divisions in multiple companies and witnessing the growth of many talented individuals. One of the most rewarding experiences was mentoring Jay, who started as an assistant project manager and is now the president of his own construction company.

When Jay joined InnovateX, he was eager to learn but lacked experience. Recognizing his potential, I took him under my wing. I provided him with challenging assignments and encouraged him to take on leadership roles within projects. I believed in the power of hands-on experience, so I made sure Jay was involved in every aspect of project management, from planning to execution.

Jay quickly demonstrated his capability and dedication. I introduced him to more complex projects, ensuring he had the support and guidance needed to succeed. Regular feedback sessions helped him refine his skills, and I encouraged him to pursue additional training and certifications.

As Jay grew in his role, I pushed him to lead his first project as the primary project manager. He excelled, delivering the project on time and within budget, while earning the respect of his team. Seeing his progress, I knew he was ready for more significant responsibilities.

Throughout his journey, I emphasized the importance of continuous learning and professional development. Jay attended leadership workshops, industry conferences, and enrolled in a construction management program. His growth was not just about acquiring skills but also about developing the confidence to lead.

Eventually, Jay's leadership abilities caught the attention of the executive team, and he was promoted to project manager. His projects consistently exceeded expectations, and he became a role model for others in the division. Jay's success story inspired many of his peers to pursue their own development paths.

Years later, Jay reached out to share that he had taken on the role of president at a construction company. Hearing this news filled me with immense pride. Developing future leaders like Jay has been one of the most fulfilling aspects of my career.

This experience underscored the importance of investing in the development of future leaders. By providing opportunities, mentorship, and continuous support, we can help talented individuals reach their full potential and make significant contributions to the industry.

Introduction

Developing future leaders is critical for ensuring the long-term success and sustainability of any organization. In a rapidly changing and increasingly complex business environment, organizations need leaders who can navigate uncertainty, drive innovation, and inspire others. This chapter explores the principles of leadership development, examines the role of talent management, and provides strategies for identifying, nurturing, and retaining future leaders. By understanding and applying these principles and strategies, organizations can build a strong pipeline of capable and visionary leaders.

The Importance of Leadership Development

Leadership development involves the systematic and intentional process of identifying, nurturing, and preparing individuals to take on leadership roles within an organization. Effective leadership development is essential for ensuring continuity, fostering innovation, and maintaining a competitive edge (Riggio, 2018).

Benefits of Leadership Development

Developing future leaders offers numerous benefits for organizations, including:

- **Enhanced Performance:** Leaders who are well-prepared and capable can drive higher levels of performance, productivity, and engagement within their teams.
- **Succession Planning:** A strong leadership pipeline ensures that the organization has qualified candidates ready to step into key roles, minimizing disruptions and maintaining continuity.
- **Employee Retention:** Investing in leadership development can enhance employee satisfaction and retention by providing growth and advancement opportunities.

- **Organizational Resilience:** Leaders who are adaptable and resilient can help the organization navigate challenges and uncertainties more effectively (Sull, 1999).

Challenges in Leadership Development

Despite its importance, leadership development presents several challenges. These include identifying high-potential individuals, providing relevant and effective development opportunities, and measuring the impact of development programs. Organizations must address these challenges to build a robust leadership pipeline (Dallas, 2015).

The Role of Talent Management

Talent management involves the strategic process of attracting, developing, and retaining skilled and capable employees. Effective talent management is crucial for leadership development, as it ensures that the organization has the right people with the right skills in the right roles (Manciagli, 2016).

Components of Talent Management

Key components of talent management include:

- **Talent Acquisition:** Identifying and attracting high-potential individuals who have the potential to become future leaders.
- **Talent Development:** Providing opportunities for growth and development, including training, mentorship, and career advancement.
- **Performance Management:** Assessing and managing employee performance to ensure alignment with organizational goals and identify development needs.
- **Succession Planning:** Developing a plan for identifying and preparing future leaders to fill key roles within the organization (Riggio, 2018).

Principles of Leadership Development

Effective leadership development is guided by key principles that ensure the process is strategic, inclusive, and sustainable. These principles provide a framework for developing future leaders who can drive organizational success.

1. Identify High-Potential Individuals

Identifying high-potential individuals is the first step in leadership development. High-potential individuals are those who demonstrate the ability to take on greater responsibility and leadership roles in the future (Sull, 1999).

Characteristics of High-Potential Individuals

High-potential individuals often exhibit the following characteristics:

- **Performance:** Consistently high levels of performance and achievement in their current roles.
- **Learning Agility:** The ability to learn quickly, adapt to new situations, and apply knowledge effectively.
- **Leadership Skills:** Strong interpersonal skills, the ability to inspire and motivate others, and a demonstrated capacity for leadership.
- **Drive and Ambition:** A strong desire for growth, advancement, and continuous improvement (Dallas, 2015).

Methods for Identifying High-Potential Individuals

Organizations can use various methods to identify high-potential individuals, including:

- **Performance Reviews:** Regular performance reviews and evaluations to assess employee performance and potential.
- **Assessment Centers:** Structured assessment centers that use simulations, exercises, and tests to evaluate leadership potential.

- **360-Degree Feedback:** Feedback from peers, subordinates, and supervisors to gain a comprehensive view of an individual's capabilities and potential.
- **Talent Reviews:** Regular talent review meetings where leaders discuss and evaluate the potential of employees across the organization (Manciagli, 2016).

2. Provide Comprehensive Development Opportunities

Providing comprehensive development opportunities is essential for nurturing future leaders. Development programs should address both technical and soft skills and be tailored to the individual needs and career aspirations of high-potential individuals (Riggio, 2018).

Components of Leadership Development Programs

Effective leadership development programs typically include the following components:

- **Formal Training:** Structured training programs that cover key leadership skills, such as communication, decision-making, and strategic thinking.
- **On-the-Job Learning:** Opportunities for hands-on learning and practical experience through challenging assignments, projects, and job rotations.
- **Mentorship and Coaching:** One-on-one mentorship and coaching relationships that provide personalized guidance, support, and feedback.
- **Networking and Exposure:** Opportunities to network with senior leaders, industry experts, and peers, and to gain exposure to different parts of the organization (Sull, 1999).

Designing Leadership Development Programs

Design leadership development programs that align with the organization's goals and address the specific needs of high-potential individuals. Consider the following steps:

- **Needs Assessment:** Conduct a needs assessment to identify the skills and competencies required for future leadership roles. Use surveys, interviews, and performance data to gather insights.
- **Curriculum Development:** Develop a comprehensive curriculum that includes a mix of formal training, experiential learning, and mentorship. Ensure that the curriculum addresses both technical and soft skills.
- **Individual Development Plans:** Create individual development plans (IDPs) for high-potential individuals, outlining specific development goals, activities, and timelines.
- **Evaluation and Feedback:** Establish mechanisms for evaluating the effectiveness of development programs and providing ongoing feedback to participants. Use metrics such as participant feedback, performance improvements, and career progression to assess impact (Dallas, 2015).

3. Foster a Culture of Continuous Learning

A culture of continuous learning is essential for leadership development. Organizations must create an environment where employees are encouraged to seek out learning opportunities, take risks, and continuously improve their skills (Manciagli, 2016).

Promoting Continuous Learning

Promote continuous learning by implementing the following practices:

- **Learning and Development Programs:** Offer a variety of learning and development programs, including workshops, seminars, online courses, and certifications. Provide opportunities for employees to pursue both formal and informal learning.
- **Encourage Self-Directed Learning:** Encourage employees to take ownership of their own learning and development. Provide access to resources such as books, articles, and online learning platforms.

- **Learning Communities:** Create learning communities or networks where employees can share knowledge, exchange ideas, and collaborate on learning initiatives. Use tools such as discussion forums, webinars, and social media to facilitate collaboration.
- **Recognize and Reward Learning:** Recognize and reward employees who demonstrate a commitment to continuous learning and development. Implement recognition programs, awards, and incentives to encourage a learning culture (Riggio, 2018).

4. Develop Emotional Intelligence

Emotional intelligence (EI) is a critical component of effective leadership. Leaders with high emotional intelligence are better able to understand and manage their own emotions, empathize with others, and build strong relationships (Sull, 1999).

Components of Emotional Intelligence

Emotional intelligence consists of several key components:

- **Self-Awareness:** The ability to recognize and understand one's own emotions, strengths, and weaknesses.
- **Self-Regulation:** The ability to manage and control one's emotions, behaviors, and impulses.
- **Motivation:** A strong drive to achieve goals, take initiative, and persist in the face of challenges.
- **Empathy:** The ability to understand and share the feelings of others, and to respond with compassion and understanding.
- **Social Skills:** The ability to build and maintain positive relationships, communicate effectively, and work collaboratively with others (Dallas, 2015).

Developing Emotional Intelligence

Organizations can help develop emotional intelligence in future leaders through the following strategies:

- **Training Programs:** Offer training programs focused on developing emotional intelligence skills, such as self-awareness, empathy, and social skills.
- **Coaching and Mentorship:** Provide coaching and mentorship to help individuals develop and apply emotional intelligence in their leadership roles. Use tools such as 360-degree feedback and self-assessment to identify areas for improvement.
- **Reflective Practice:** Encourage reflective practice by promoting regular self-reflection and feedback. Use techniques such as journaling, mindfulness, and peer feedback to enhance self-awareness and emotional regulation (Manciagli, 2016).

5. Encourage Diversity and Inclusion

Diversity and inclusion are essential for effective leadership development. Diverse leadership teams bring a range of perspectives, experiences, and ideas, enhancing decision-making and innovation (Riggio, 2018).

Benefits of Diversity and Inclusion

Encouraging diversity and inclusion in leadership development offers several benefits, including:

- **Enhanced Innovation:** Diverse teams are more likely to generate creative and innovative solutions to complex problems.
- **Better Decision-Making:** Diverse perspectives lead to more comprehensive and well-informed decision-making.
- **Improved Employee Engagement:** Inclusive cultures foster a sense of belonging and engagement among employees, leading to higher levels of motivation and retention.
- **Increased Organizational Performance:** Organizations with diverse and inclusive leadership teams tend to perform better financially and achieve higher levels of customer satisfaction (Sull, 1999).

Strategies for Encouraging Diversity and Inclusion

Implement the following strategies to encourage diversity and inclusion in leadership development:

- **Inclusive Recruitment:** Develop inclusive recruitment practices to attract diverse talent. Use diverse interview panels and ensure that job descriptions are inclusive and free from bias.
- **Diverse Talent Pools:** Build diverse talent pools by identifying and nurturing high-potential individuals from underrepresented groups. Use talent reviews and succession planning to ensure diversity in leadership pipelines.
- **Inclusive Development Programs:** Design leadership development programs that address the unique needs and experiences of diverse individuals. Provide training on unconscious bias, cultural competence, and inclusive leadership.
- **Mentorship and Sponsorship:** Establish mentorship and sponsorship programs to support the development of diverse talent. Pair diverse individuals with senior leaders who can provide guidance, support, and advocacy (Dallas, 2015).

6. Implement Effective Succession Planning

Succession planning involves identifying and preparing individuals to take on key leadership roles within the organization. Effective succession planning ensures continuity, minimizes disruptions, and supports long-term organizational success (Manciagli, 2016).

Components of Succession Planning

Effective succession planning includes the following components:

- **Identify Critical Roles:** Identify key leadership roles that are critical to the organization's success. Focus on roles that have a significant impact on strategy, operations, and performance.

- **Assess Potential Successors:** Assess potential successors for critical roles based on their performance, potential, and readiness. Use tools such as talent reviews, assessments, and development plans to evaluate candidates.
- **Develop Successors:** Provide targeted development opportunities to prepare successors for their future roles. Use a combination of formal training, on-the-job learning, mentorship, and coaching.
- **Monitor and Adjust Plans:** Regularly review and update succession plans to ensure they remain relevant and effective. Monitor the progress of potential successors and make adjustments as needed (Riggio, 2018).

Steps for Implementing Succession Planning

Implement succession planning through the following steps:

- **Conduct a Talent Audit:** Conduct a talent audit to identify current and future leadership needs. Assess the organization's strengths, weaknesses, and gaps in leadership talent.
- **Develop Succession Profiles:** Create succession profiles for key leadership roles, outlining the skills, competencies, and experiences required for success. Use these profiles to guide the assessment and development of potential successors.
- **Create Development Plans:** Develop individual development plans (IDPs) for potential successors, outlining specific development goals, activities, and timelines. Provide support and resources to help candidates achieve their development goals.
- **Review and Update Plans:** Conduct regular reviews of succession plans to assess progress and make necessary adjustments. Use feedback and performance data to inform decisions and ensure that succession plans remain aligned with organizational goals (Sull, 1999).

7. Measure and Evaluate Leadership Development

Measuring and evaluating leadership development efforts is essential for understanding their impact and making data-driven decisions. Organizations must establish metrics and evaluation processes to track the effectiveness of leadership development programs (Dallas, 2015).

Leadership Development Metrics

Establish metrics to measure the success of leadership development efforts, including:

- **Participation Rates:** Track the number of employees participating in leadership development programs.
- **Completion Rates:** Measure the completion rates of leadership development programs and activities.
- **Performance Improvements:** Assess improvements in performance and behavior among participants, using metrics such as performance reviews, feedback, and assessments.
- **Career Progression:** Track the career progression of participants, including promotions, role changes, and advancements.
- **Employee Engagement:** Measure the impact of leadership development on employee engagement and satisfaction, using surveys and feedback.
- **Organizational Performance:** Evaluate the long-term impact of leadership development on organizational performance, including metrics such as revenue growth, profitability, and customer satisfaction (Manciagli, 2016).

Evaluation Processes

Implement evaluation processes to assess the effectiveness of leadership development programs:

- **Regular Reviews:** Conduct regular reviews of leadership development programs to track progress and identify areas for improvement. Use a combination of quantitative data and qualitative insights to evaluate performance.

- **Feedback Loops:** Establish feedback loops to gather input from participants, mentors, and other stakeholders. Use feedback to refine and improve leadership development programs.
- **Continuous Improvement:** Use the insights gained from measurement and evaluation to drive continuous improvement. Implement best practices and lessons learned to enhance future leadership development efforts (Riggio, 2018).

The Role of Transformational Leadership in Developing Future Leaders

Transformational leadership is essential for developing future leaders within an organization. Transformational leaders inspire and motivate their teams, create a vision for the future, and foster a culture of continuous improvement and development (Sull, 1999).

Characteristics of Transformational Leaders

Transformational leaders possess several key characteristics that enable them to develop future leaders:

Vision: Transformational leaders have a clear and compelling vision for the future. They communicate this vision with passion and enthusiasm, inspiring others to join them on the journey.

Inspiration: Transformational leaders inspire their teams by setting high expectations and challenging them to achieve their full potential. They provide encouragement and support, fostering a sense of purpose and commitment.

Intellectual Stimulation: Transformational leaders encourage creativity, innovation, and critical thinking. They challenge the status quo and promote a culture of continuous learning and improvement.

Individualized Consideration: Transformational leaders show genuine concern for the needs and development of their followers. They provide personalized support and mentorship, helping employees grow and succeed (Dallas, 2015).

Strategies for Developing Transformational Leadership

Organizations can develop transformational leadership by implementing targeted development programs and creating a supportive environment for transformational behaviors (Manciagli, 2016).

Leadership Development Programs

Implement leadership development programs that focus on developing the skills and behaviors associated with transformational leadership. These programs should cover areas such as visioning, communication, emotional intelligence, and change management. Use a mix of classroom training, experiential learning, and coaching to develop well-rounded transformational leaders (Riggio, 2018).

Mentorship and Coaching

Provide mentorship and coaching to emerging leaders to support their development. Pair experienced transformational leaders with high-potential employees to facilitate knowledge transfer and skill development. Use coaching to provide personalized feedback and guidance, helping leaders refine their transformational behaviors (Sull, 1999).

Creating a Supportive Environment

Create an environment that supports and encourages transformational leadership behaviors. This includes fostering a culture of trust, collaboration, and innovation. Recognize and reward leaders who demonstrate transformational behaviors, and provide opportunities for them to share their experiences and insights with others (Dallas, 2015).

Strategies for Developing Future Leaders

Developing future leaders requires a strategic and structured approach. The following strategies provide a roadmap for organizations to build and sustain a robust leadership pipeline.

1. Implement a Leadership Development Framework

A leadership development framework provides a structured approach for identifying, developing, and retaining future leaders. This framework ensures that leadership development efforts are aligned with organizational goals and are systematically managed (Manciagli, 2016).

Components of a Leadership Development Framework

- **Leadership Competencies:** Define the key competencies required for leadership roles within the organization. Use these competencies to guide the development of leadership programs and the assessment of potential leaders.
- **Development Programs:** Develop a portfolio of leadership development programs that address the needs of leaders at different levels. Include a mix of formal training, on-the-job learning, mentorship, and coaching.
- **Talent Management Processes:** Integrate leadership development with talent management processes, such as performance management, succession planning, and career development. Ensure that leadership development is embedded in the organization's overall talent strategy.
- **Measurement and Evaluation:** Establish metrics and evaluation processes to track the effectiveness of leadership development efforts. Use data to inform decisions and drive continuous improvement (Riggio, 2018).

2. Create Individual Development Plans

Individual development plans (IDPs) provide a personalized roadmap for the development of future leaders. IDPs outline specific development goals, activities, and timelines, and provide a clear path for growth and advancement (Sull, 1999).

Developing Individual Development Plans

- **Assessment:** Conduct an assessment of the individual's current skills, competencies, and development needs. Use tools such as performance reviews, 360-degree feedback, and self-assessment to gather insights.
- **Goal Setting:** Set clear, specific, and measurable development goals that align with the individual's career aspirations and the organization's leadership competencies.
- **Development Activities:** Identify and plan development activities that will help the individual achieve their goals. Include a mix of formal training, on-the-job learning, mentorship, and coaching.
- **Progress Tracking:** Establish mechanisms for tracking progress and providing ongoing feedback. Use regular check-ins, performance reviews, and development discussions to assess progress and make adjustments as needed (Dallas, 2015).

3. Provide Opportunities for Stretch Assignments

Stretch assignments provide high-potential individuals with challenging and meaningful experiences that develop their leadership skills and capabilities. These assignments push individuals out of their comfort zones and expose them to new perspectives and responsibilities (Manciagli, 2016).

Types of Stretch Assignments

- **Cross-Functional Projects:** Assign individuals to cross-functional projects that require collaboration and coordination across different departments. These projects provide exposure to different parts of the organization and develop skills in teamwork, communication, and strategic thinking.

- **International Assignments:** Provide opportunities for international assignments that involve working in different countries and cultures. These assignments develop global leadership skills, cultural competence, and adaptability.
- **Special Projects:** Assign individuals to special projects that address critical business challenges or strategic initiatives. These projects provide opportunities for innovation, problem-solving, and strategic decision-making.
- **Interim Roles:** Assign individuals to interim roles where they can take on leadership responsibilities temporarily. These roles provide hands-on experience in managing teams, making decisions, and driving performance (Riggio, 2018).

4. Foster a Mentorship Culture

Mentorship is a powerful tool for developing future leaders. A strong mentorship culture provides high-potential individuals with guidance, support, and opportunities for growth and development (Sull, 1999).

Building a Mentorship Culture

- **Formal Mentorship Programs:** Establish formal mentorship programs that pair high-potential individuals with experienced leaders. Provide training and resources to support mentors and mentees in their relationships.
- **Informal Mentorship Opportunities:** Encourage informal mentorship relationships by creating a culture of support and collaboration. Provide opportunities for networking and relationship-building.
- **Mentorship Training:** Provide training for mentors on effective mentoring techniques and practices. Offer workshops, resources, and tools to help mentors develop their skills.

- **Recognition and Rewards:** Recognize and reward mentors who contribute to the development of future leaders. Implement recognition programs and awards to celebrate successful mentorship relationships (Dallas, 2015).

5. Develop a Culture of Feedback

A culture of feedback is essential for continuous improvement and development. Organizations must create an environment where feedback is regularly given and received, and where individuals are encouraged to learn and grow from feedback (Manciagli, 2016).

Promoting a Culture of Feedback

- **Regular Feedback:** Provide regular feedback to individuals on their performance, behaviors, and development. Use a combination of formal and informal feedback mechanisms.
- **Constructive Feedback:** Ensure that feedback is constructive, specific, and actionable. Focus on behaviors and outcomes, and provide suggestions for improvement.
- **Feedback Training:** Provide training for leaders and employees on giving and receiving feedback effectively. Offer workshops, resources, and tools to develop feedback skills.
- **Feedback Tools:** Use feedback tools, such as 360-degree feedback, performance reviews, and self-assessment, to gather comprehensive feedback from multiple sources (Riggio, 2018).

6. Encourage Lifelong Learning

Lifelong learning is essential for the continuous development of future leaders. Organizations must create an environment where employees are encouraged to pursue learning opportunities throughout their careers (Sull, 1999).

Supporting Lifelong Learning

- **Learning Opportunities:** Provide a wide range of learning opportunities, including workshops, seminars, online courses, certifications, and conferences. Encourage employees to pursue both formal and informal learning.

- **Learning Resources:** Provide access to learning resources, such as books, articles, videos, and online learning platforms. Create a library of resources that employees can use to support their learning.
- **Learning Goals:** Encourage employees to set personal learning goals and create individual learning plans. Provide support and resources to help employees achieve their learning goals.
- **Recognition and Rewards:** Recognize and reward employees who demonstrate a commitment to lifelong learning. Implement recognition programs, awards, and incentives to encourage continuous learning (Dallas, 2015).

7. Measure and Evaluate Leadership Development

Measuring and evaluating leadership development efforts is essential for understanding their impact and making data-driven decisions. Organizations must establish metrics and evaluation processes to track the effectiveness of leadership development programs (Manciagli, 2016).

Leadership Development Metrics

Establish metrics to measure the success of leadership development efforts, including:

- **Participation Rates:** Track the number of employees participating in leadership development programs.
- **Completion Rates:** Measure the completion rates of leadership development programs and activities.
- **Performance Improvements:** Assess improvements in performance and behavior among participants, using metrics such as performance reviews, feedback, and assessments.
- **Career Progression:** Track the career progression of participants, including promotions, role changes, and advancements.

- **Employee Engagement:** Measure the impact of leadership development on employee engagement and satisfaction, using surveys and feedback.
- **Organizational Performance:** Evaluate the long-term impact of leadership development on organizational performance, including metrics such as revenue growth, profitability, and customer satisfaction (Riggio, 2018).

Evaluation Processes

Implement evaluation processes to assess the effectiveness of leadership development programs:

- **Regular Reviews:** Conduct regular reviews of leadership development programs to track progress and identify areas for improvement. Use a combination of quantitative data and qualitative insights to evaluate performance.
- **Feedback Loops:** Establish feedback loops to gather input from participants, mentors, and other stakeholders. Use feedback to refine and improve leadership development programs.
- **Continuous Improvement:** Use the insights gained from measurement and evaluation to drive continuous improvement. Implement best practices and lessons learned to enhance future leadership development efforts (Sull, 1999).

Case Studies: Developing Future Leaders

Examining real-world examples of organizations that have successfully developed future leaders provides valuable insights and inspiration.

Case Study 1: General Electric

General Electric (GE) has long been recognized for its leadership development programs. GE's commitment to developing future leaders is evident in its comprehensive approach, which includes formal training, on-the-job learning, mentorship, and succession planning. The company's focus on leadership development has produced many successful leaders who have gone on to lead GE and other organizations (Dallas, 2015).

Case Study 2: IBM

IBM's leadership development programs emphasize continuous learning, innovation, and global experience. The company's focus on developing leaders who can navigate complex and dynamic environments has been instrumental in its success. IBM's leadership development initiatives include cross-functional projects, international assignments, and a strong mentorship culture (Manciagli, 2016).

Case Study 3: Google

Google's leadership development programs are designed to foster a culture of innovation and continuous improvement. The company provides a wide range of development opportunities, including formal training, on-the-job learning, and mentorship. Google's commitment to diversity and inclusion is also reflected in its leadership development efforts, which aim to build a diverse pipeline of future leaders (Riggio, 2018).

Conclusion

Developing future leaders is critical for ensuring the long-term success and sustainability of any organization. By understanding and applying the principles and strategies outlined in this chapter, organizations can build a strong pipeline of capable and visionary leaders.

The case studies of General Electric, IBM, and Google demonstrate the power of effective leadership development and the benefits of a strategic, inclusive approach. These organizations have successfully developed future leaders by fostering a culture of continuous learning, providing comprehensive development opportunities, and implementing effective talent management and succession planning processes.

By adopting the strategies outlined in this chapter, organizations can enhance their leadership development efforts and ensure a bright future. Embracing a culture of feedback, encouraging lifelong learning, and leveraging transformational leadership will enable organizations to develop leaders who can navigate uncertainty, drive innovation, and inspire others.

References

Benedict, A. (2007). 2007 change management survey report. Alexandria, VA: Society for Human Resource Management.

Dallas, H. J. (2015, October 22). Here are 4 ways leaders can deal with change. *Fortune*. Retrieved from http://fortune.com/2015/10/22/change-leaders-managers/

Manciagli, D. (2016, April 13). 4 biggest challenges facing business leaders today. *Biz Journals*. Retrieved from https://www.bizjournals.com/bizjournals/how-to/growth-strategies/2016/04/4-biggest-challenges-facing-business-leaders-today.html

Riggio, R. E. (2018, December 9). What is servant leadership and why does it matter? *Psychology Today*. Retrieved from https://www.psychologytoday.com/us/blog/cutting-edge-leadership/201812/what-is-servant-leadership-and-why-does-it-matter

Sull, D. (1999, July-August). Why good companies go bad. *Harvard Business Review*, 42–55. Retrieved from https://hbr.org/1999/07/why-good-companies-go-bad

CHAPTER 13

The Path to Sustained Success Through Adaptation, Innovation, and Leadership

Introduction

The journey of navigating change, fostering innovation, and developing leadership is a continuous process that demands dedication, foresight, and strategic thinking. This book has explored the multifaceted nature of organizational adaptation, the pivotal role of technology, the importance of cultivating a resilient culture, and the critical need for effective leadership and innovation. In this conclusion, we will synthesize the key themes and insights from the preceding chapters, offering a comprehensive framework for organizations aiming to achieve sustained success in an ever-evolving business landscape.

Embracing Change and Adaptation

In the contemporary business environment, change is the only constant. Organizations that thrive are those that embrace change proactively rather than reactively. The ability to adapt to new circumstances, whether they be technological advancements, market shifts, or regulatory changes, is paramount.

The Nature of Organizational Adaptation

Organizational adaptation involves the capacity to evolve in response to external and internal pressures. This evolution can be incremental or transformational, but it must always be strategic. The key to successful adaptation lies in understanding the driving forces of change and developing a strategic response that aligns with the organization's goals and values (Riggio, 2018).

Strategies for Effective Adaptation

To effectively adapt, organizations must:

- **Foster a Culture of Agility:** Create an organizational culture that values flexibility, responsiveness, and continuous learning. Encourage employees to embrace change and view it as an opportunity for growth.
- **Leverage Data and Analytics:** Use data-driven insights to inform decision-making and anticipate future trends. Invest in technologies that enable real-time analytics and predictive modeling.
- **Engage Stakeholders:** Involve key stakeholders in the adaptation process. Solicit input and feedback from employees, customers, partners, and other relevant parties to ensure a comprehensive understanding of the change landscape.
- **Develop Resilience:** Build organizational resilience by enhancing operational efficiency, fostering innovation, and investing in employee well-being. Resilient organizations are better equipped to navigate disruptions and capitalize on emerging opportunities (Sull, 1999).

Case Study: Netflix

Netflix's transformation from a DVD rental service to a global streaming giant exemplifies successful adaptation. By embracing technological advancements and shifting consumer preferences, Netflix has continuously evolved its business model and offerings, maintaining a competitive edge in the entertainment industry (Dallas, 2015).

The Role of Technology in Driving Change

Technology is a powerful enabler of organizational adaptation and innovation. It can enhance operational efficiency, support data-driven decision-making, and open new avenues for growth and value creation.

Key Technological Trends

Several technological trends are shaping the business landscape and driving organizational change:

- **Artificial Intelligence (AI) and Machine Learning:** AI and machine learning technologies enable organizations to automate processes, enhance decision-making, and develop innovative products and services.
- **Big Data and Analytics:** The ability to collect, analyze, and interpret vast amounts of data provides organizations with valuable insights into customer behavior, market trends, and operational performance.
- **Cloud Computing:** Cloud computing offers scalable, flexible, and cost-effective solutions for data storage, processing, and collaboration. It supports remote work and enhances organizational agility.
- **Internet of Things (IoT):** IoT technologies connect physical devices to the internet, enabling real-time monitoring, control, and data collection. This enhances operational efficiency and supports predictive maintenance.
- **Blockchain:** Blockchain technology provides a secure and transparent way to record transactions and track assets, with applications in various industries, including finance, supply chain management, and healthcare (Manciagli, 2016).

Strategies for Leveraging Technology

To effectively leverage technology, organizations should:

- **Align Technology with Business Goals:** Ensure that technology investments support the organization's strategic objectives. Develop a technology roadmap that aligns with long-term goals.
- **Invest in Digital Transformation:** Embrace digital transformation by adopting new technologies and upgrading legacy systems. Develop digital capabilities and foster a culture of innovation.
- **Enhance Data Management and Security:** Implement robust data governance frameworks and invest in cybersecurity measures to protect sensitive information and ensure compliance with data protection regulations.
- **Build Digital Skills:** Invest in training and development programs to equip employees with the skills needed to leverage new technologies effectively. Foster a culture of continuous learning and innovation (Riggio, 2018).

Case Study: Amazon

Amazon's relentless focus on technological innovation has been a key driver of its success. From its use of AI in recommendation systems to its investment in cloud computing through AWS, Amazon continues to leverage technology to enhance customer experience and drive growth (Sull, 1999).

Cultivating a Resilient Organizational Culture

A resilient organizational culture is essential for navigating uncertainty and achieving sustained success. Resilience enables organizations to withstand challenges, adapt to changing conditions, and seize new opportunities.

Components of Organizational Resilience

Key components of organizational resilience include:

- **Adaptability and Agility:** The ability to adjust strategies, structures, and processes in response to changing conditions.

- **Employee Engagement and Well-being:** Engaged and well-supported employees are more committed, motivated, and capable of handling stress and uncertainty.
- **Strong Leadership:** Effective leaders set the tone for the organization, guiding its response to challenges and fostering a culture of resilience.
- **Continuous Learning and Innovation:** A culture of continuous learning and innovation enhances the organization's ability to navigate disruptions and capitalize on emerging opportunities (Dallas, 2015).

Strategies for Fostering Resilience

To foster organizational resilience, leaders should:

- **Articulate a Compelling Vision:** Communicate a clear and compelling vision that aligns the organization's efforts and inspires commitment.
- **Build a Strong Leadership Team:** Form a cohesive leadership team with diverse perspectives and expertise to drive the transformation effort.
- **Engage and Empower Employees:** Involve employees in the transformation process and provide opportunities for input and participation.
- **Foster a Culture of Innovation:** Encourage experimentation, risk-taking, and continuous improvement, creating an environment where new ideas can flourish.
- **Implement Effective Change Management Practices:** Develop a structured approach to managing change, addressing resistance, and ensuring smooth transitions.
- **Monitor and Evaluate Progress:** Establish metrics for tracking progress, conduct regular reviews, and make adjustments as needed.

- **Sustain the Transformation:** Reinforce new behaviors, continuously improve practices, and maintain a focus on long-term goals (Manciagli, 2016).

Case Study: Johnson & Johnson

Johnson & Johnson's response to the Tylenol crisis in the 1980s is a classic example of organizational resilience. The company's swift and transparent actions, including a nationwide recall and the introduction of tamper-resistant packaging, restored public trust and reinforced its resilient culture (Riggio, 2018).

The Role of Transformational Leadership

Transformational leadership is crucial for guiding organizations through significant changes and fostering a culture of innovation and continuous improvement.

Characteristics of Transformational Leaders

Transformational leaders possess several key characteristics:

- **Vision:** They have a clear and compelling vision for the future and can communicate it effectively to inspire others.
- **Inspiration:** They set high expectations and challenge their teams to achieve their full potential, providing encouragement and support.
- **Intellectual Stimulation:** They encourage creativity, innovation, and critical thinking, promoting a culture of continuous learning and improvement.
- **Individualized Consideration:** They show genuine concern for the needs and development of their followers, providing personalized support and mentorship (Sull, 1999).

Strategies for Developing Transformational Leadership

Organizations can develop transformational leadership through:

- **Leadership Development Programs:** Implement programs that focus on visioning, communication, emotional intelligence, and change management. Use a mix of classroom training, experiential learning, and coaching.
- **Mentorship and Coaching:** Provide mentorship and coaching to emerging leaders, facilitating knowledge transfer and skill development. Use tools such as 360-degree feedback and self-assessment.
- **Creating a Supportive Environment:** Foster a culture of trust, collaboration, and innovation. Recognize and reward leaders who demonstrate transformational behaviors (Dallas, 2015).

Case Study: Microsoft

Microsoft's transformation under CEO Satya Nadella exemplifies the impact of transformational leadership. By shifting the company's focus to cloud computing and fostering a culture of innovation and collaboration, Nadella has led Microsoft to new heights (Manciagli, 2016).

Building and Sustaining Innovation

Innovation is essential for driving growth, enhancing competitiveness, and responding to changing market demands. Building and sustaining innovation requires a strategic and structured approach.

Principles of Innovation

Effective innovation is guided by key principles:

- **Foster a Culture of Innovation:** Create an environment that supports creativity, experimentation, and continuous improvement. Encourage employees to contribute new ideas.

- **Align Innovation with Strategic Goals:** Ensure that innovation efforts are aligned with the organization's strategic objectives and priorities.
- **Provide Resources and Support:** Invest in the tools, training, and funding needed to drive innovation. Provide opportunities for hands-on learning and practical experience.
- **Implement Effective Innovation Processes:** Establish structured processes for managing innovation, from idea generation to commercialization.
- **Encourage Collaboration and Open Innovation:** Leverage external partnerships and networks to enhance innovation efforts.
- **Measure and Evaluate Innovation:** Establish metrics and evaluation processes to track the performance of innovation initiatives (Riggio, 2018).

Strategies for Implementing and Managing Innovation

To build and sustain innovation, organizations should:

- **Establish an Innovation Strategy:** Develop a clear framework for guiding innovation efforts, including vision, priorities, and objectives.
- **Create an Innovation Ecosystem:** Build a network of internal and external stakeholders to support and enhance innovation efforts.
- **Implement Agile and Lean Methodologies:** Use structured approaches for managing innovation projects, emphasizing iterative development and continuous improvement.
- **Develop a Robust Idea Management System:** Capture, evaluate, and implement new ideas systematically.
- **Leverage Technology and Digital Tools:** Invest in the right tools and technologies to support the development and implementation of new ideas.

- **Foster a Learning Organization:** Encourage continuous learning, knowledge sharing, and innovation throughout the organization (Sull, 1999).

Case Study: 3M

3M's innovation strategy has led to the development of iconic products such as Post-it Notes and Scotch Tape. The company fosters a culture of innovation by encouraging employees to dedicate time to exploring new ideas and providing the resources and support needed to drive innovation (Dallas, 2015).

Developing Future Leaders

Developing future leaders is critical for ensuring the long-term success and sustainability of any organization. Effective leadership development involves identifying high-potential individuals, providing comprehensive development opportunities, and fostering a culture of continuous learning and improvement.

Principles of Leadership Development

Effective leadership development is guided by key principles:

- **Identify High-Potential Individuals:** Identify individuals who demonstrate the ability to take on greater responsibility and leadership roles.
- **Provide Comprehensive Development Opportunities:** Offer a mix of formal training, on-the-job learning, mentorship, and coaching.
- **Foster a Culture of Continuous Learning:** Encourage employees to seek out learning opportunities and continuously improve their skills.
- **Develop Emotional Intelligence:** Help future leaders develop self-awareness, self-regulation, motivation, empathy, and social skills.

- **Encourage Diversity and Inclusion:** Build diverse and inclusive leadership teams to enhance decision-making and innovation.
- **Implement Effective Succession Planning:** Identify and prepare individuals to take on key leadership roles.
- **Measure and Evaluate Leadership Development:** Establish metrics and evaluation processes to track the effectiveness of leadership development efforts (Manciagli, 2016).

Strategies for Developing Future Leaders

To develop future leaders, organizations should:

- **Implement a Leadership Development Framework:** Provide a structured approach for identifying, developing, and retaining future leaders.
- **Create Individual Development Plans:** Provide personalized development plans that outline specific goals, activities, and timelines.
- **Provide Opportunities for Stretch Assignments:** Offer challenging and meaningful experiences that develop leadership skills and capabilities.
- **Foster a Mentorship Culture:** Create a strong mentorship culture that provides guidance, support, and opportunities for growth.
- **Develop a Culture of Feedback:** Encourage regular, constructive feedback to promote continuous improvement and development.
- **Encourage Lifelong Learning:** Create an environment where employees are encouraged to pursue learning opportunities throughout their careers.
- **Measure and Evaluate Leadership Development:** Track the success of leadership development efforts and make data-driven decisions to drive continuous improvement (Riggio, 2018).

Case Study: IBM

IBM's leadership development programs emphasize continuous learning, innovation, and global experience. The company's focus on developing leaders who can navigate complex and dynamic environments has been instrumental in its success (Dallas, 2015).

Synthesizing Key Insights

Throughout this book, we have explored the critical elements of organizational adaptation, innovation, and leadership development. The following key insights provide a comprehensive framework for achieving sustained success:

1. Embrace Change Proactively

Organizations must view change as an opportunity rather than a threat. Proactively embracing change enables organizations to stay ahead of the curve and capitalize on emerging opportunities.

2. Leverage Technology Strategically

Technology is a powerful enabler of change and innovation. Organizations must strategically invest in and leverage technology to enhance operational efficiency, support data-driven decision-making, and drive innovation.

3. Foster a Resilient Culture

A resilient culture is essential for navigating uncertainty and achieving sustained success. Organizations must cultivate adaptability, engage and support employees, and foster a culture of continuous learning and improvement.

4. Develop Transformational Leaders

Transformational leaders inspire and motivate their teams, create a vision for the future, and foster a culture of innovation and continuous improvement. Organizations must develop and support transformational leaders to drive successful change and innovation.

5. Build and Sustain Innovation

Innovation is essential for driving growth and enhancing competitiveness. Organizations must create a culture that supports innovation, provide the necessary resources and support, and implement structured processes for managing innovation.

6. Develop Future Leaders

Developing future leaders is critical for ensuring the long-term success and sustainability of any organization. Organizations must identify high-potential individuals, provide comprehensive development opportunities, and foster a culture of continuous learning and improvement.

Conclusion

Achieving sustained success in today's dynamic and complex business environment requires a strategic and holistic approach. By embracing change, leveraging technology, fostering a resilient culture, developing transformational leaders, building and sustaining innovation, and developing future leaders, organizations can navigate uncertainty, drive growth, and achieve long-term success.

The journey of organizational adaptation, innovation, and leadership development is continuous and ever-evolving. By applying the principles and strategies outlined in this book, leaders can guide their organizations through the challenges and opportunities of the modern business landscape, ensuring a bright and successful future.

References

Benedict, A. (2007). 2007 change management survey report. Alexandria, VA: Society for Human Resource Management.

Dallas, H. J. (2015, October 22). Here are 4 ways leaders can deal with change. *Fortune*. Retrieved from http://fortune.com/2015/10/22/change-leaders-managers/

Manciagli, D. (2016, April 13). 4 biggest challenges facing business leaders today. *Biz Journals*. Retrieved from https://www.bizjournals.com/bizjournals/how-to/growth-strategies/2016/04/4-biggest-challenges-facing-business-leaders-today.html

Riggio, R. E. (2018, December 9). What is servant leadership and why does it matter? *Psychology Today*. Retrieved from https://www.psychologytoday.com/us/blog/cutting-edge-leadership/201812/what-is-servant-leadership-and-why-does-it-matter

Sull, D. (1999, July-August). Why good companies go bad. *Harvard Business Review*, 42–55. Retrieved from https://hbr.org/1999/07/why-good-companies-go-bad

CHAPTER 14

Conclusion - The Path Forward

As we reach the conclusion of this book, it's important to reflect on the journey we've taken together through the multifaceted world of organizational success. From embracing change and leveraging technology to fostering innovation and developing future leaders, we've explored the essential strategies that can propel any organization toward sustained success. Each chapter has built upon the last, forming a comprehensive guide for navigating the complexities of today's dynamic business environment.

Embracing Change and Adaptation

Change is the only constant in the business world. Organizations that thrive are those that embrace change proactively, seeing it not as a threat but as an opportunity for growth and improvement. The ability to adapt to new circumstances—whether they be technological advancements, market shifts, or regulatory changes—is paramount. By fostering a culture of agility and resilience, organizations can navigate uncertainties with confidence and poise.

Leveraging Technology for Growth

Technology is a powerful enabler of innovation and efficiency. The stories of adopting Procore and iPads in the field or integrating AI and big data analytics illustrate how technology can transform operations, enhance decision-making, and drive competitive advantage. Organizations that strategically invest in and leverage technology are better equipped to respond to market demands, improve customer experiences, and streamline internal processes.

Fostering a Culture of Innovation

Innovation is the lifeblood of sustained success. It requires creating an environment where creativity is encouraged, risk-taking is supported, and new ideas are nurtured. The success of modular construction techniques and the establishment of an "Innovation Fund" highlight the importance of investing in innovative practices and maintaining an open mind to new approaches. By fostering a culture of continuous improvement and embracing innovative solutions, organizations can stay ahead of the curve and drive long-term growth.

Developing Resilient and Adaptable Leaders

Effective leadership is crucial for guiding organizations through periods of change and uncertainty. Leaders must not only be strategic thinkers but also empathetic communicators and resilient problem-solvers. The development of future leaders like Jay underscores the importance of mentorship, continuous learning, and providing opportunities for growth. Organizations that invest in their people and prioritize leadership development will build a strong pipeline of capable leaders ready to tackle future challenges.

Building a Cohesive and Inclusive Culture

A cohesive and inclusive culture is essential for attracting and retaining top talent. Organizations that value diversity and inclusion, promote open communication, and foster a sense of belonging will benefit from a more engaged and motivated workforce. The experiences shared throughout this book demonstrate the positive impact of a supportive and inclusive environment on employee satisfaction and organizational performance.

Strategic Decision-Making and Flexibility

In times of uncertainty, strategic decision-making and flexibility are critical. Organizations must be able to assess risks, prioritize key initiatives, and pivot when necessary. The stories of navigating downturns and leading through rebranding efforts illustrate the importance of being adaptable and making informed decisions. By staying focused on long-term goals while remaining flexible in the face of change, organizations can build resilience and sustain success.

The Role of Continuous Learning

Continuous learning is the cornerstone of personal and organizational growth. Encouraging employees to seek out new knowledge, develop new skills, and stay current with industry trends fosters a culture of lifelong learning. This not only enhances individual performance but also drives organizational innovation and adaptability. Providing access to training, development programs, and learning resources is essential for building a workforce that is prepared for the future.

Conclusion

The path to organizational success is not a straight line; it is a journey filled with challenges, opportunities, and continuous learning. By embracing change, leveraging technology, fostering innovation, developing leaders, building a cohesive culture, making strategic decisions, and promoting continuous learning, organizations can navigate the complexities of the modern business landscape and achieve sustained success.

The stories and strategies shared in this book are just the beginning. As you move forward, remember that the key to success lies in your ability to adapt, innovate, and lead with purpose and vision. By applying the principles outlined in these chapters, you can build a resilient, dynamic, and successful organization capable of thriving in an ever-evolving world.

Thank you for joining me on this journey. I hope the insights and experiences shared in these pages inspire you to take bold steps, embrace change, and lead your organization to new heights. The future is yours to shape—go forth and make it extraordinary.

References

This reference section compiles all the sources cited throughout the book, providing comprehensive and coherent documentation of the research, theories, and case studies that have informed the principles and strategies discussed. Proper referencing ensures credibility and allows readers to further explore the concepts presented.

Books and Book Chapters

Kotter, J. P. (1996). *Leading Change.* Harvard Business Review Press.

In this seminal work, John Kotter outlines an eight-step process for leading successful change initiatives within organizations. His framework emphasizes the importance of creating a sense of urgency, building guiding coalitions, and anchoring new approaches in the organizational culture.

Northouse, P. G. (2018). *Leadership: Theory and Practice* (8th ed.). Sage Publications.

Northouse's comprehensive textbook covers a wide range of leadership theories and practices. It provides insights into transformational leadership, servant leadership, and the development of leadership skills, which are essential for fostering innovation and guiding organizational transformation.

Schein, E. H. (2017). *Organizational Culture and Leadership* (5th ed.). Wiley.

Edgar Schein explores the dynamics of organizational culture and its impact on leadership effectiveness. His work emphasizes the role of leaders in shaping and changing organizational culture to support adaptation and innovation.

Tushman, M. L., & O'Reilly, C. A. (2013). *Winning Through Innovation: A Practical Guide to Leading Organizational Change and Renewal.* Harvard Business Review Press.

Tushman and O'Reilly provide a practical guide for leaders seeking to drive innovation and organizational renewal. Their book offers frameworks and strategies for balancing exploration and exploitation, managing ambidextrous organizations, and sustaining innovation over the long term.

Ulrich, D., Smallwood, N., & Sweetman, K. (2009). *The Leadership Code: Five Rules to Lead By*. Harvard Business Press.

This book presents a leadership framework based on five essential rules for effective leadership: shaping the future, making things happen, engaging today's talent, building the next generation, and investing in yourself. These rules provide a foundation for developing future leaders.

Journal Articles and Papers

Brown, S. L., & Eisenhardt, K. M. (1997). The Art of Continuous Change: Linking Complexity Theory and Time-Paced Evolution in Relentlessly Shifting Organizations. *Administrative Science Quarterly, 42*(1), 1-34.

This article explores how organizations can achieve continuous change by linking complexity theory with time-paced evolution. The authors highlight the importance of balancing stability and change to maintain organizational effectiveness.

Christensen, C. M., Raynor, M. E., & McDonald, R. (2015). What Is Disruptive Innovation? *Harvard Business Review, 93*(12), 44-53.

Christensen and his colleagues provide a detailed explanation of disruptive innovation and its implications for organizations. Their work emphasizes the need for companies to recognize and respond to disruptive forces in their industries.

Drucker, P. F. (2002). The Discipline of Innovation. *Harvard Business Review, 80*(8), 95-102.

Peter Drucker discusses the discipline required for effective innovation. He identifies key principles and practices that organizations must adopt to foster a culture of innovation and drive continuous improvement.

Heifetz, R. A., & Laurie, D. L. (1997). The Work of Leadership. *Harvard Business Review, 75*(1), 124-134.

Adaptive Leadership

Heifetz and Laurie explore the concept of adaptive leadership, which involves guiding organizations through complex and uncertain environments. Their article provides insights into how leaders can mobilize people to tackle tough challenges and thrive in times of change.

Ries, E. (2011). The Lean Startup: How Today's Entrepreneurs Use Continuous Innovation to Create Radically Successful Businesses. *Crown Business.*

Eric Ries introduces the Lean Startup methodology, which emphasizes rapid experimentation, validated learning, and iterative development. This approach is particularly relevant for fostering innovation and adapting to changing market conditions.

Reports and White Papers

McKinsey & Company. (2018). *The Business Value of Design.* McKinsey & Company.

This report highlights the importance of design in driving business performance. McKinsey & Company provides evidence-based insights into how design excellence can enhance customer experience, support innovation, and create competitive advantage.

PwC. (2017). *Global CEO Survey: 20 Years Inside the Mind of the CEO... What's Next?.* PwC.

PwC's annual CEO survey explores the perspectives of global business leaders on key trends, challenges, and opportunities. The 2017 edition provides valuable insights into how CEOs are navigating technological disruption, geopolitical uncertainty, and changing customer expectations.

World Economic Forum. (2016). *The Future of Jobs: Employment, Skills and Workforce Strategy for the Fourth Industrial Revolution.* World Economic Forum.

This report examines the impact of the Fourth Industrial Revolution on employment, skills, and workforce strategies. It provides insights into the skills required for future jobs and the implications for education and training systems.

Web Articles and Blog Posts

Davenport, T. H., & Kirby, J. (2016, March). Just How Smart Are Smart Machines? *Harvard Business Review*. Retrieved from https://hbr.org/2016/03/just-how-smart-are-smart-machines

Davenport and Kirby explore the capabilities and limitations of smart machines, including artificial intelligence and machine learning. Their article provides a balanced perspective on the potential and challenges of these technologies.

Goleman, D. (2015, April). Emotional Intelligence: Why It Can Matter More Than IQ. *LinkedIn*. Retrieved from https://www.linkedin.com/pulse/emotional-intelligence-why-can-matter-more-than-iq-daniel-goleman

Daniel Goleman discusses the importance of emotional intelligence in leadership. He explains how self-awareness, self-regulation, motivation, empathy, and social skills contribute to effective leadership and organizational success.

Hamel, G. (2012, November). What Matters Now: How to Win in a World of Relentless Change, Ferocious Competition, and Unstoppable Innovation. *Harvard Business Review*. Retrieved from https://hbr.org/2012/11/what-matters-now-how-to-win-in-a-world-of-relentless-change-ferocious-competition-and-unstoppable-innovation

Gary Hamel explores the key priorities for organizations in a rapidly changing world. He emphasizes the need for innovation, adaptability, and a focus on values to drive long-term success.

Kanter, R. M. (2011, October). How Great Companies Think Differently. *Harvard Business Review*. Retrieved from https://hbr.org/2011/10/how-great-companies-think-differently

Rosabeth Moss Kanter examines the distinguishing characteristics of great companies. She highlights the importance of purpose, values, and a long-term perspective in shaping successful and resilient organizations.

McGrath, R. G. (2013, January). Transient Advantage. *Harvard Business Review*. Retrieved from https://hbr.org/2013/01/transient-advantage

Rita McGrath introduces the concept of transient advantage, arguing that competitive advantages are increasingly temporary. She provides strategies for building and sustaining success in a dynamic and fast-paced business environment.

Books and E-Books

Covey, S. R. (2004). *The 7 Habits of Highly Effective People: Powerful Lessons in Personal Change*. Free Press.

Stephen Covey's classic book provides a framework for personal and professional effectiveness. His seven habits offer timeless principles for achieving success and leading a meaningful life.

Grant, A. (2016). *Originals: How Non-Conformists Move the World.* Viking.

Adam Grant explores the traits and behaviors of original thinkers who drive innovation and change. His book offers insights into how individuals and organizations can foster creativity and challenge the status quo.

Pink, D. H. (2011). *Drive: The Surprising Truth About What Motivates Us*. Riverhead Books.

Daniel Pink examines the factors that drive human motivation, challenging traditional notions of incentives and rewards. His book provides a fresh perspective on how to inspire and engage employees.

Sinek, S. (2009). *Start With Why: How Great Leaders Inspire Everyone to Take Action*. Portfolio.

Simon Sinek's book emphasizes the importance of starting with "why" to inspire and motivate others. He explains how great leaders and organizations create a sense of purpose and drive sustained success.

Zenger, J. H., & Folkman, J. (2019). *The New Extraordinary Leader: Turning Good Managers into Great Leaders.* McGraw-Hill Education.

Zenger and Folkman provide a research-based approach to developing extraordinary leaders. Their book offers practical strategies for enhancing leadership effectiveness and driving organizational performance.

Online Courses and Webinars

Coursera. (n.d.). *Leading People and Teams Specialization.* University of Michigan. Retrieved from https://www.coursera.org/specializations/leading-people-teams

This Coursera specialization, offered by the University of Michigan, covers key concepts and skills for effective leadership. The courses focus on topics such as motivating people, managing talent, and leading teams.

Harvard Online. (n.d.). *Leadership Principles.* Harvard Business School Online. Retrieved from https://online.hbs.edu/courses/leadership-principles/

Harvard Business School Online offers a course on leadership principles, providing insights into effective leadership practices and strategies. The course covers topics such as emotional intelligence, decision-making, and leading change.

LinkedIn Learning. (n.d.). *Developing Executive Presence.* LinkedIn Learning. Retrieved from https://www.linkedin.com/learning/developing-executive-presence

This LinkedIn Learning course focuses on developing executive presence, a critical aspect of effective leadership. The course covers topics such as communication skills, confidence, and personal branding.

Udemy. (n.d.). *Mastering Organizational Change Management.* Udemy. Retrieved from https://www.udemy.com/course/mastering-organizational-change-management/

Udemy offers a course on mastering organizational change management, providing practical tools and techniques for leading change initiatives. The course covers topics such as change planning, communication, and overcoming resistance.

edX. (n.d.). *Innovation and Creativity Management.* RWTH Aachen University. Retrieved from https://www.edx.org/course/innovation-and-creativity-management

RWTH Aachen University's course on edX explores the principles and practices of innovation and creativity management. The course provides insights into fostering a culture of innovation and developing creative solutions to business challenges.

Podcasts and Audio Books

Brown, B. (Host). (2018-present). *Dare to Lead.* Spotify. Retrieved from https://open.spotify.com/show/4eZIK8j34N5Vn6tE7FoJXb

Brené Brown's podcast, Dare to Lead, features conversations with leaders, change-makers, and culture shifters. The podcast explores topics related to leadership, vulnerability, courage, and resilience.

Grove, A. (2005). *High Output Management* [Audiobook]. Audible Studios. Retrieved from https://www.audible.com/pd/High-Output-Management-Audiobook/B002VA9VRI

Andy Grove's audiobook, High Output Management, provides practical insights into effective management and leadership. Grove shares his experiences and lessons learned from leading Intel.

Hoffman, R. (Host). (2017-present). *Masters of Scale.* WaitWhat. Retrieved from https://mastersofscale.com/

Reid Hoffman's podcast, Masters of Scale, features interviews with successful entrepreneurs and business leaders. The podcast explores the principles and strategies for scaling businesses and achieving long-term success.

Klein, E. (Host). (2014-present). *The Ezra Klein Show*. Vox Media. Retrieved from https://www.vox.com/ezra-klein-show

Ezra Klein's podcast features interviews with thought leaders, policymakers, and experts on a wide range of topics, including leadership, innovation, and organizational change. The podcast provides valuable insights into contemporary issues and trends.

Williams, R. (Host). (2016-present). *The Leadership Hacker*. The Leadership Hacker Podcast. Retrieved from https://leadership-hacker.com/

The Leadership Hacker podcast, hosted by Rich Williams, features conversations with leadership experts and practitioners. The podcast covers topics such as transformational leadership, change management, and developing future leaders.

Conferences and Workshops

Harvard Business Review Leadership Summit. (n.d.). Retrieved from https://hbrleadershipsummit.hbr.org/

The Harvard Business Review Leadership Summit brings together top business leaders and thought leaders to discuss the latest trends and challenges in leadership. The summit offers valuable networking opportunities and insights into effective leadership practices.

World Business Forum. (n.d.). Retrieved from https://www.wobi.com/world-business-forum/

The World Business Forum is an annual event that features keynote speakers, panel discussions, and workshops on leadership, innovation, and organizational change. The forum provides a platform for leaders to exchange ideas and learn from industry experts.

TED Conferences. (n.d.). Retrieved from https://www.ted.com/attend/conferences

TED Conferences bring together thought leaders, innovators, and change-makers to share their ideas and experiences. TED Talks cover a wide range of topics related to leadership, innovation, and personal development.

SHRM Annual Conference & Expo. (n.d.). Retrieved from https://annual.shrm.org/

The Society for Human Resource Management (SHRM) Annual Conference & Expo is a premier event for HR professionals and leaders. The conference offers sessions on leadership development, talent management, and organizational culture.

Aspen Ideas Festival. (n.d.). Retrieved from https://www.aspenideas.org/

The Aspen Ideas Festival features discussions and presentations by thought leaders, policymakers, and experts on a wide range of topics, including leadership, innovation, and social change. The festival provides a forum for exploring new ideas and solutions to global challenges.

Websites and Online Resources

Center for Creative Leadership. (n.d.). Retrieved from https://www.ccl.org/

The Center for Creative Leadership (CCL) provides research, training, and resources for leadership development. The website offers articles, reports, and tools to help organizations develop effective leaders.

Harvard Business Review. (n.d.). Retrieved from https://hbr.org/

Harvard Business Review (HBR) is a leading source of insights and best practices on leadership, innovation, and organizational change. The website features articles, case studies, and research reports from industry experts and thought leaders.

McKinsey & Company. (n.d.). Retrieved from https://www.mckinsey.com/

McKinsey & Company is a global management consulting firm that provides research, insights, and solutions for business leaders. The website offers articles, reports, and tools on topics such as strategy, innovation, and leadership.

MIT Sloan Management Review. (n.d.). Retrieved from https://sloanreview.mit.edu/

MIT Sloan Management Review (MIT SMR) publishes research and insights on management, leadership, and innovation. The website features articles, case studies, and reports from academics and industry experts.

Society for Human Resource Management (SHRM). (n.d.). Retrieved from https://www.shrm.org/

The Society for Human Resource Management (SHRM) provides resources, tools, and training for HR professionals and leaders. The website offers articles, reports, and best practices on leadership development, talent management, and organizational culture.

Government and Industry Reports

National Institute of Standards and Technology (NIST). (2018). *Cybersecurity Framework*. NIST.

The NIST Cybersecurity Framework provides guidelines and best practices for managing cybersecurity risks. The framework helps organizations protect their critical assets and ensure the security of their information systems.

U.S. Department of Labor. (2017). *Futurework: Trends and Challenges for Work in the 21st Century.* U.S. Department of Labor.

This report examines the trends and challenges shaping the future of work in the 21st century. It provides insights into the skills and competencies required for future jobs and the implications for workforce development.

World Economic Forum. (2020). *The Global Risks Report.* World Economic Forum.

The Global Risks Report explores the major risks facing the world today, including economic, environmental, geopolitical, societal, and technological risks. The report provides insights into how organizations can build resilience and navigate uncertainty.

International Monetary Fund (IMF). (2019). *World Economic Outlook.* IMF.

The IMF's World Economic Outlook provides analysis and forecasts of global economic trends and developments. The report offers insights into the economic forces shaping the business environment and their implications for organizations.

Organization for Economic Co-operation and Development (OECD). (2021). *OECD Skills Outlook.* OECD.

The OECD Skills Outlook examines the skills needed for success in the modern economy and the policies required to support skill development. The report provides insights into how organizations can invest in workforce development and enhance their competitiveness.

Research Databases and Academic Journals

ProQuest. (n.d.). Retrieved from https://www.proquest.com/

ProQuest is a comprehensive research database that provides access to academic journals, dissertations, and other scholarly resources. It is an invaluable tool for conducting research on leadership, innovation, and organizational change.

JSTOR. (n.d.). Retrieved from https://www.jstor.org/

JSTOR is a digital library that provides access to academic journals, books, and primary sources. It offers a wealth of resources on topics related to leadership, management, and business strategy.

Google Scholar. (n.d.). Retrieved from https://scholar.google.com/

Google Scholar is a freely accessible search engine that indexes scholarly articles, theses, books, and conference papers. It is a useful resource for finding academic research and publications on leadership and innovation.

PubMed. (n.d.). Retrieved from https://pubmed.ncbi.nlm.nih.gov/

PubMed is a research database that provides access to biomedical and life sciences literature. It is a valuable resource for research on health-related leadership and organizational practices.

IEEE Xplore. (n.d.). Retrieved from https://ieeexplore.ieee.org/

IEEE Xplore is a digital library that provides access to technical literature in engineering, computer science, and related fields. It offers resources on the latest technological advancements and their applications in business and industry.

Industry Associations and Professional Organizations

Association for Talent Development (ATD). (n.d.). Retrieved from https://www.td.org/

The Association for Talent Development (ATD) is a professional organization dedicated to promoting talent development and workplace learning. The website offers resources, tools, and training for developing effective leaders and enhancing organizational performance.

International Coach Federation (ICF). (n.d.). Retrieved from https://coachfederation.org/

The International Coach Federation (ICF) is a professional organization for coaches and coaching practitioners. The website provides resources, certification programs, and best practices for leadership coaching and development.

Project Management Institute (PMI). (n.d.). Retrieved from https://www.pmi.org/

The Project Management Institute (PMI) is a professional organization for project management practitioners. The website offers resources, certifications, and training for project management and leadership development.

Society for Industrial and Organizational Psychology (SIOP). (n.d.). Retrieved from https://www.siop.org/

The Society for Industrial and Organizational Psychology (SIOP) is a professional organization for I-O psychologists and practitioners. The website provides research, tools, and best practices for enhancing leadership, performance, and organizational culture.

American Management Association (AMA). (n.d.). Retrieved from https://www.amanet.org/

The American Management Association (AMA) is a professional organization that provides training, resources, and certification programs for managers and leaders. The website offers articles, webinars, and workshops on leadership, innovation, and organizational development.

Conclusion

The references compiled in this section provide a robust foundation for the principles and strategies discussed throughout this book. By drawing on a diverse range of sources, including books, journal articles, reports, online resources, and industry best practices, we have ensured that the insights and recommendations presented are well-supported and grounded in research.

These references offer valuable resources for further exploration and learning, enabling leaders to deepen their understanding of the topics covered and apply these insights to their own organizations. As the business landscape continues to evolve, staying informed and continuously learning will be key to achieving sustained success through adaptation, innovation, and leadership.

References

Benedict, A. (2007). 2007 change management survey report. Alexandria, VA: Society for Human Resource Management.

Dallas, H. J. (2015, October 22). Here are 4 ways leaders can deal with change. *Fortune*. Retrieved from http://fortune.com/2015/10/22/change-leaders-managers/

Manciagli, D. (2016, April 13). 4 biggest challenges facing business leaders today. *Biz Journals*. Retrieved from https://www.bizjournals.com/bizjournals/how-to/growth-strategies/2016/04/4-biggest-challenges-facing-business-leaders-today.html

Riggio, R. E. (2018, December 9). What is servant leadership and why does it matter? *Psychology Today*. Retrieved from https://www.psychologytoday.com/us/blog/cutting-edge-leadership/201812/what-is-servant-leadership-and-why-does-it-matter

Sull, D. (1999, July-August). Why good companies go bad. *Harvard Business Review*, 42–55. Retrieved from https://hbr.org/1999/07/why-good-companies-go-bad

Appendices

The appendices section provides supplementary information that supports the concepts and strategies discussed in the book. This includes detailed frameworks, tools, templates, and additional resources that leaders can use to implement the principles outlined in the chapters.

Appendix A: Change Management Framework

The change management framework outlined in this appendix provides a structured approach for guiding organizations through transformational change. It includes key phases, activities, and tools to support effective change management.

1. Define the Change Vision and Objectives

- **Vision Statement:** Craft a clear and compelling vision statement that describes the desired future state of the organization.
- **Objectives:** Define specific, measurable objectives that align with the vision and provide a roadmap for achieving the desired outcomes.

2. Assess the Current State

- **SWOT Analysis:** Conduct a SWOT analysis to assess the organization's strengths, weaknesses, opportunities, and threats.
- **Stakeholder Analysis:** Identify key stakeholders and assess their influence, interests, and potential impact on the change initiative.

3. Develop the Change Plan

- **Change Strategy:** Develop a change strategy that outlines the key initiatives, timelines, and resources required to achieve the change objectives.
- **Communication Plan:** Create a communication plan to ensure transparent and effective communication with all stakeholders throughout the change process.

4. Implement the Change

- **Action Plans:** Develop detailed action plans for each initiative, including specific tasks, responsibilities, and timelines.
- **Change Agents:** Identify and train change agents who will champion the change and support their colleagues through the transition.

5. Monitor and Evaluate Progress

- **Performance Metrics:** Establish metrics to measure the progress and success of the change initiatives. Use these metrics to track performance and identify areas for improvement.
- **Feedback Mechanisms:** Implement feedback mechanisms to gather input from stakeholders and make necessary adjustments to the change plan.

6. Sustain the Change

- **Reinforcement:** Reinforce new behaviors and practices through recognition, rewards, and ongoing training.
- **Continuous Improvement:** Promote a culture of continuous improvement by encouraging employees to identify and implement enhancements to processes and practices.

Appendix B: Innovation Toolkit

The innovation toolkit provides practical tools and techniques to support the development and implementation of innovative ideas. These tools can be used to facilitate brainstorming, evaluate ideas, and manage innovation projects.

1. Brainstorming Techniques

- **Mind Mapping:** Use mind mapping to visually organize ideas and explore connections between different concepts.
- **SCAMPER:** Apply the SCAMPER technique (Substitute, Combine, Adapt, Modify, Put to another use, Eliminate, Reverse) to generate new ideas by altering existing products or processes.
- **Reverse Brainstorming:** Identify potential problems and obstacles to innovation and then brainstorm solutions to overcome them.

2. Idea Evaluation Tools

- **Idea Scoring Matrix:** Develop an idea scoring matrix to evaluate ideas based on criteria such as feasibility, market potential, and alignment with strategic goals.
- **SWOT Analysis:** Conduct a SWOT analysis for each idea to assess its strengths, weaknesses, opportunities, and threats.
- **Cost-Benefit Analysis:** Perform a cost-benefit analysis to determine the potential return on investment for each idea.

3. Innovation Management Processes

- **Stage-Gate Process:** Implement a stage-gate process to manage innovation projects, with defined stages and decision points to evaluate progress and determine whether to proceed.
- **Agile Methodology:** Use agile methodologies to manage innovation projects, emphasizing iterative development, continuous feedback, and flexibility.

- **Lean Startup:** Apply lean startup principles, such as validated learning, build-measure-learn cycles, and minimum viable products (MVPs), to rapidly develop and test new ideas.

Appendix C: Leadership Development Templates

The leadership development templates provide structured formats for creating individual development plans (IDPs), conducting performance reviews, and implementing mentorship programs.

1. Individual Development Plan (IDP) Template

Name: [Employee Name]

Position: [Current Position]

Development Goals:

1. [Goal 1]
2. [Goal 2]
3. [Goal 3]

Development Activities:

1. [Activity 1]
   - Description: [Brief Description]
   - Timeline: [Start Date - End Date]
   - Resources: [Required Resources]
2. [Activity 2]
   - Description: [Brief Description]
   - Timeline: [Start Date - End Date]
   - Resources: [Required Resources]

3. [Activity 3]
   - Description: [Brief Description]
   - Timeline: [Start Date - End Date]
   - Resources: [Required Resources]

Progress Tracking:

- [Milestone 1]
- [Milestone 2]
- [Milestone 3]

Feedback and Support:

- Mentor/Coach: [Name]
- Feedback Mechanisms: [Description]

2. Performance Review Template

Employee Name: [Employee Name]

Position: [Current Position]

Review Period: [Start Date - End Date]

Performance Summary:

- Strengths: [List of Strengths]
- Areas for Improvement: [List of Areas for Improvement]

Goals and Achievements:

1. [Goal 1]
   - Achievement: [Description]
   - Rating: [Rating]

2. [Goal 2]
    - o Achievement: [Description]
    - o Rating: [Rating]
1. [Goal 3]
    - o Achievement: [Description]
    - o Rating: [Rating]

Development Plan:

- Short-Term Goals: [List of Goals]
- Long-Term Goals: [List of Goals]
- Development Activities: [List of Activities]

Feedback and Comments:

- Employee Feedback: [Comments]
- Manager Feedback: [Comments]

3. Mentorship Program Template

Mentorship Program Overview:

- Program Objectives: [Objectives]
- Duration: [Program Duration]
- Eligibility: [Eligibility Criteria]

Mentor Information:

- Name: [Mentor Name]
- Position: [Mentor Position]
- Contact Information: [Contact Details]

Mentee Information:

- Name: [Mentee Name]
- Position: [Mentee Position]
- Contact Information: [Contact Details]

Mentorship Plan:

- Goals: [List of Goals]
- Activities: [List of Activities]
- Timeline: [Start Date - End Date]

Meeting Schedule:

- Frequency: [Meeting Frequency]
- Duration: [Meeting Duration]
- Agenda: [Meeting Agenda]

Feedback and Evaluation:

- Feedback Mechanisms: [Description]
- Evaluation Criteria: [Criteria]

Appendix D: Additional Resources

This appendix provides a list of additional resources, including books, articles, websites, and organizations, that offer valuable insights and tools for leaders seeking to enhance their skills and drive organizational success.

Books:

1. **Collins, J.** (2001). *Good to Great: Why Some Companies Make the Leap... and Others Don't.* HarperBusiness.

2. **Dweck, C. S.** (2006). *Mindset: The New Psychology of Success.* Random House.

3. **Heath, C., & Heath, D.** (2010). *Switch: How to Change Things When Change Is Hard.* Crown Business.

4. **Lencioni, P.** (2002). *The Five Dysfunctions of a Team: A Leadership Fable.* Jossey-Bass.

5. **Zenger, J. H., & Folkman, J.** (2002). *The Extraordinary Leader: Turning Good Managers into Great Leaders.* McGraw-Hill.

Articles:

1. **Christensen, C. M., & Overdorf, M.** (2000). Meeting the Challenge of Disruptive Change. *Harvard Business Review, 78*(2), 66-76.

2. **Hamel, G., & Prahalad, C. K.** (1994). Competing for the Future. *Harvard Business Review, 72*(4), 122-128.

3. **Kotter, J. P.** (2007). Leading Change: Why Transformation Efforts Fail. *Harvard Business Review, 85*(1), 96-103.

4. **Senge, P. M.** (1990). The Leader's New Work: Building Learning Organizations. *Sloan Management Review, 32*(1), 7-23.

5. **Ulrich, D., & Smallwood, N.** (2004). Capitalizing on Capabilities. *Harvard Business Review, 82*(6), 119-127.

Websites:

1. **American Management Association (AMA):** https://www.amanet.org/

2. **Center for Creative Leadership (CCL):** https://www.ccl.org/

3. **Harvard Business Review (HBR):** https://hbr.org/

4. **McKinsey & Company:** https://www.mckinsey.com/

5. **Society for Human Resource Management (SHRM):** https://www.shrm.org/

Organizations:

1. **Association for Talent Development (ATD):** https://www.td.org/
2. **International Coach Federation (ICF):** https://coachfederation.org/
3. **Project Management Institute (PMI):** https://www.pmi.org/
4. **Society for Industrial and Organizational Psychology (SIOP):** https://www.siop.org/
5. **World Economic Forum (WEF):** https://www.weforum.org/

Appendix E: Case Study Summaries

This appendix provides summaries of the case studies discussed in the book. These case studies illustrate real-world examples of successful organizational adaptation, innovation, and leadership development.

Case Study: Netflix

Overview: Netflix transformed from a DVD rental service to a global streaming giant by embracing technological advancements and shifting consumer preferences. The company's continuous evolution of its business model and offerings has enabled it to maintain a competitive edge in the entertainment industry.

Key Strategies:

- Embracing digital transformation and investing in streaming technology.
- Adapting to changing consumer behaviors and preferences.

- Innovating with original content production to differentiate from competitors.

Case Study: Amazon

Overview: Amazon's relentless focus on technological innovation has driven its success. From its use of AI in recommendation systems to its investment in cloud computing through AWS, Amazon continues to leverage technology to enhance customer experience and drive growth.

Key Strategies:

- Leveraging data analytics and AI to personalize customer experiences.
- Expanding into cloud computing with Amazon Web Services (AWS).
- Continuously innovating and expanding product and service offerings.

Case Study: Johnson & Johnson

Overview: Johnson & Johnson's response to the Tylenol crisis in the 1980s is a classic example of organizational resilience. The company's swift and transparent actions, including a nationwide recall and the introduction of tamper-resistant packaging, restored public trust and reinforced its resilient culture.

Key Strategies:

- Prioritizing customer safety and transparent communication during the crisis.
- Implementing tamper-resistant packaging to enhance product safety.
- Reinforcing a culture of resilience and commitment to customer well-being.

Case Study: Microsoft

Overview: Microsoft's transformation under CEO Satya Nadella exemplifies the impact of transformational leadership. By shifting the company's focus to cloud computing and fostering a culture of innovation and collaboration, Nadella has led Microsoft to new heights.

Key Strategies:

- Fostering a growth mindset and culture of continuous learning.
- Shifting the company's focus to cloud computing and AI technologies.
- Promoting collaboration and innovation across the organization.

Case Study: 3M

Overview: 3M's innovation strategy has led to the development of iconic products such as Post-it Notes and Scotch Tape. The company fosters a culture of innovation by encouraging employees to dedicate time to exploring new ideas and providing the resources and support needed to drive innovation.

Key Strategies:

- Encouraging employees to spend 15% of their time on personal innovation projects.
- Investing in research and development to drive product innovation.
- Creating a supportive environment that fosters creativity and experimentation.

Appendix F: Glossary of Key Terms

This appendix provides definitions of key terms and concepts discussed in the book. Understanding these terms is essential for applying the principles and strategies outlined in the chapters.

Adaptive Leadership: A leadership approach that focuses on guiding organizations through complex and uncertain environments by mobilizing people to tackle tough challenges and thrive in times of change.

Agile Methodology: A project management approach that emphasizes iterative development, continuous feedback, and flexibility to adapt to changing requirements and deliver value quickly.

Artificial Intelligence (AI): The simulation of human intelligence processes by machines, particularly computer systems, to perform tasks such as learning, reasoning, and problem-solving.

Blockchain: A decentralized digital ledger technology that provides a secure and transparent way to record transactions and track assets, with applications in various industries.

Change Management: The process of planning, implementing, and monitoring changes within an organization to ensure a smooth transition and achieve desired outcomes.

Continuous Improvement: An ongoing effort to enhance processes, products, or services by making incremental improvements and fostering a culture of innovation and learning.

Emotional Intelligence (EI): The ability to recognize, understand, and manage one's own emotions, as well as the emotions of others, to build strong relationships and make effective decisions.

Innovation Ecosystem: A network of internal and external stakeholders, including employees, customers, partners, and suppliers, that supports and enhances innovation efforts.

Lean Startup: A methodology for developing businesses and products that emphasizes rapid experimentation, validated learning, and iterative development to reduce risk and increase success.

Organizational Resilience: The capacity of an organization to withstand and recover from challenges, adapt to changing conditions, and seize new opportunities.

Succession Planning: The process of identifying and preparing individuals to take on key leadership roles within an organization to ensure continuity and long-term success.

Transformational Leadership: A leadership style that inspires and motivates followers to achieve extraordinary outcomes by creating a compelling vision, fostering innovation, and promoting continuous improvement.

Conclusion

The appendices provide practical tools, frameworks, and additional resources to support the implementation of the principles and strategies discussed throughout the book. By utilizing these appendices, leaders can enhance their ability to navigate change, foster innovation, and develop future leaders, ultimately driving sustained success for their organizations.

Printed in the USA
CPSIA information can be obtained
at www.ICGtesting.com
LVHW050537240924
791763LV00001B/1